K'uei Hsing

A REPOSITORY OF ASIAN LITERATURE IN TRANSLATION

INDIANA UNIVERSITY EAST ASIAN SERIES

K'UEI HSING

A REPOSITORY OF ASIAN LITERATURE
IN TRANSLATION / EDITED BY

Liu Wu-chi   *F. A. Bischoff*
Jerome P. Seaton   *Kenneth Yasuda*

FOR THE INTERNATIONAL AFFAIRS CENTER
Indiana University Press / Bloomington & London

This book was brought to publication with support from Ford Foundation funds made available through the Office of Research and Advanced Studies, Indiana University.

COVER CALLIGRAPHY BY CHIANG YEE

Copyright © 1974 by Indiana University Press

ALL RIGHTS RESERVED

No part of this book may be reproduced or utilized in any form or by any means, electronic or mechanical, including photocopying and recording, or by any information storage and retrieval system, without permission in writing from the publisher. The Association of American University Presses Resolution on Permissions constitutes the only exception to this prohibition.

PUBLISHED IN CANADA BY FITZHENRY & WHITESIDE LIMITED,
DON MILLS, ONTARIO

Library of Congress catalog card number: 74-149799 | ISNB: 253-39101-6

Manufactured in the United States of America

The poems by Tanikawa Shuntarō "Love for Paul Klee" and "Request" © 1971 by Harold P. Wright; "Sadness II" and "Sonnet 45" © 1972 by Harold P. Wright.

The following poems by Hsin Ch'i-chi were included in *Hsin Ch'i-chi* by Irving Yucheng Lo (Twayne, 1971), with credit to the present volume, first announced for 1971 but subsequently delayed: A 1, 2, 4; B 1, 2; C 1, 4, 6 (part); D 2, 3, 5-7; E 1, 3, 4, 7; F 2.

CONTENTS

FOREWORD by F. A. BISCHOFF   vii
INTRODUCTION by LIU WU-CHI   ix

from the Chinese

Lu In (Lu Yin) THE THIRTEEN EXTANT POEMS /
    HUGH M. STIMSON   1
Ssu-ma Kuang INSTRUCTIONS ON FRUGALITY FOR MY
    SON K'ANG / A. S. SARITI   11
Hsiang Hsiu FU ON REMEMBERING THE PAST /
    ROGER BAILEY   17
Hsin Ch'i-chi THIRTY LYRICS BY "A POET'S POET" /
    IRVING YUCHENG LO   21
Wang Yü-ch'eng THE BAMBOO PAVILION-TOWER
    OF HUANG-KANG / JAN W. WALLS   67
Tzu-yeh SONGS OF THE FOUR SEASONS: SPRING & SUMMER /
    MICHAEL WORKMAN   71
Lao She NEIGHBORS / WILLIAM A. LYELL, JR.   81
Wang Kai FROM THE MUSTARD SEED GARDEN MANUAL OF
    PAINTING / HENRY W. WELLS   97

from the Japanese

SEVEN TALES OF YAMATO / GERALD B. MATHIAS   107
Tanikawa Shuntarō FOUR POEMS / HAROLD WRIGHT   121
Kusano Shimpei THREE POEMS WITH SOUNDS & REPORT OF A
    CERTAIN DEATH / KAMAIKE SUSUMA &
    CID CORMAN   127

from the Oirat-Mongolian

THE MANUHARI JĀTAKA-TALE / JOHN R. KRUEGER 137

from the Tibetan

Chaṅs-dbyaṅs Rgya-mcho SELECTIONS FROM THE LOVE POETRY OF THE SIXTH DALAI LAMA / CHARLES HARTMAN 167

THE GOBLIN K'UEI HSING by F. A. BISCHOFF 171

NOTE: *Each translation is preceded by an Introduction or introductory note by the translator, whose name appears after the slash in each entry above.*

FOREWORD

Our decision to develop a repository of East and Central Asian literature grew from our observation that men of Asian letters tend to be skilled amateurs in the first meaning of the word—persons whose incentive is *l'art pour l'art*. Such persons tend to have at least one or two well-made translations languishing in a desk drawer. We hope to rescue any such works and to stimulate others.

This volume of *K'uei Hsing* is a trial balloon and has allowed considerable variety in methods of translation as well as in the extent of commentary and annotation. If our adventures are successful, we trust that other volumes will follow, each subsequent volume specific in theme.

The story is told of a Chinese scholar named K'uei, as famous for his literary talent as for the deformity of his face, who attained first rank in the Literary Examinations at the Capital. It was customary for the Emperor to present, with his own hand, a golden rose to the lucky candidate. Therefore, according to the ritual, K'uei stepped forward to receive the reward that was due to him. But the Emperor, repelled by his ugly face, refused to bestow on him the golden rose. Heartbroken, the poor scholar went off to drown himself. When he was about to expire at the bottom of the river, a mysterious fish named Ngao took him upon its back and returned him to the surface. K'uei then ascended to heaven and became a star (*hsing*) and was worshipped as the Patron of Literature. His palace is located in the square of the Big Dipper.

This is the explanation of our somewhat cryptic title.

K'uei Hsing is not intended to be a scholarly publication in the strict sense of the word, but rather to provide leisurely and enjoyable reading for scholars and artists who, led by their curiosity, have discovered the charms of Central and East Asian cultures. May K'uei Hsing's Repository encourage us to enjoy more assiduously the puzzle of the quadrature of the circle, to which Max Müller compared the rendering of Oriental texts into a Western language.

F. A. BISCHOFF

INTRODUCTION

In the realm of literature the universal language of humanity can transcend all differences of nationality, historical period, genre, and taste. The literatures of East and Central Asia extend and enrich this language, but they are presently almost unknown to the people of the modern West. The publication of this first volume of *K'uei Hsing* is an attempt to introduce Western readers to the remarkable diversity and complexity, as well as to the humanity, of Eastern literary traditions. China, Japan, Mongolia, and Tibet are represented here in a wide variety of ancient and modern literary forms encompassing poetry, the short story, essay, folk song, and Jātaka tale, but our initial emphasis is on Chinese poetry.

K'uei Hsing opens with the *shih* poems of Lu In, a ninth-century writer who died in such poverty that his funeral had to be paid for by a friend and patron. Also included are a wide selection from the *tz'u* lyrics of Hsin Ch'i-chi, a twelfth-century poet much admired by his countrymen for his erudition and versatility; and forty of the somewhat less elegant but highly symbolic fourth-century love songs of Tzu-yeh (Lady Midnight). The *fu*, or prose-poem of Hsiang Hsiu (third century), one of the Seven Sages of the Bamboo Grove, laments the passing of his dead friends, seeing his own fate in theirs. The last poem in this section is a rendering in English verse from a Chinese manual on the art of painting, originally written in prose. That such an exercise occurred to a skilled translator suggests that a poetic quality of the Chinese language may occasionally highlight a book of practical instruction.

Selections from two modern Japanese poets are included. The translation of four poems by the young poet Tanikawa Shuntarō reveals the strongly Western influence in his art. An American poet has collaborated in a free rendition of Kusano Shimpei, an ultra-modern among moderns. In contrast, the example of Tibetan love poetry was composed by the august leader, the Sixth Dalai Lama.

The prose selections in this volume are equally diverse. Ssu-ma Kuang's instructions to his son expound the moral virtues of frugality. The writer is an eminent eleventh-century Confucian historian. The charm of the intriguing descriptive essay on a bamboo pavilion, written in 999 by Wang Yu-ch'eng, an official in exile, is matched only by the poignancy of its symbolism. The seven folk tales from ancient Japan (mid-tenth century) were considered by scholars of their day to be "frivolous women's stuff," yet they are among the few examples of popular prose writing to have survived from that time. The Mongolian tale of the Jātaka type translated here tells of the great Buddha in one of his previous incarnations; throughout the story, the faithful gain in devotion and understanding. And from the pen of Lao Shê, the author of *The Rickshaw Boy*, comes a modern tale, rich in irony, about two bourgeois Chinese couples.

The diversity of materials and contents in this volume is matched by the diversity in the techniques and methods of translation employed by the contributors. Their several approaches to the translation of poetry may cast some light on the knotty problems of translation. All translation involves risks and compromises which in unskilled hands can misrepresent the original. Perhaps nowhere else is this difficulty more obvious than in Chinese poetry since each Chinese poem (*shih* or *tz'u*), while restricted to a fixed number of words in each line, is governed by strict rules of prosody such as the alternation of words in opposite tonal patterns, the use of caesuras, balanced expressions, end-rhymes, alliterations, etc.

To illustrate in more detail the prosody and rhyme scheme of the Chinese poem, poem E4 by Hsin Ch'i-chi is shown below in three stages of translation. The original form of the poem in Chinese characters is followed by a modern Mandarin transliteration. Tonal marks are added to the transliterated version which follows the Wade-Giles system. These marks, ¯ ´ ˇ ` , indicate the first, second, third, and fourth tones. The word-for-word translation is given below each line. Where a compound occurs, necessitating the use of only one English word, or where grammatical particles are left out, the equivalent terms appear in a parenthesis. The tune-pattern ("West River Moon/*Hsi-chiang-yüeh*") of this poem has two stanzas, each of which contains four lines, six characters in lines one, two, and four, and seven characters in line three. The rhyme scheme requires that three of the four lines rhyme but with two different sets of rhyme-words—one in the "even" tone (*i.e.*, the first or second tones) and the other in an "oblique" tone (*i.e.*, the third or the fourth tones). Thus, using a lower-case letter to indicate a rhyme-word from the oblique tone group and an upper-case letter to indicate a rhyme-word from the even tone group (with x standing for unrhymed words), the form of this tune-pattern can be diagrammed as:

$$\begin{array}{cccc cccc} 6 & 6 & 7 & 6 // & 6 & 6 & 7 & 6 \\ x & A & A & b & x & A & A & b \end{array}$$

醉裏且貪歡笑
要愁那得工夫
近來始覺古人書
信著全無是處

昨夜松邊醉倒
問松我醉何如
只疑松動要來扶
以手推松曰去

tsùi drunk	*lǐ* (in-midst-of)	*ch'ieh* why-not	*t'an* to covet	*huan-* merriment	*hsiào* laughing	
yào about-to	*ch'óu* to grieve	*nǎ* where	*té* to find	*kūng-* (time)	*fū*	
chìn (recently)	*lái*	*shǐh* to begin	*chüéh* to feel	*kǔ-* (the ancients')	*jén*	*shū* book
hsìn to believe	*ché* (auxiliary word)	*ch'üán* completely	*wú* there-is-no	*shìh* true	*ch'ù* place	
tsó- last	*yèh* night	*sūng* pine tree	*pien* alongside	*tsùi-* to become drunk	*tǎo* to lie down	
wèn to ask	*sūng* pine tree	*wǒ* I (or) my	*tsùi* drunkenness	*hó* (how-is-it-like)	*jú*	
chǐh only	*í* to suspect or fear	*sūng* pine tree	*tùng* to move	*yaò* about-to	*lái* come	*fú* lift-up
ǐ with	*shǒu* hand	*t'ūi* to push	*sūng* pine tree	*yüēh* say	*ch'ù* to go away	

The task of the translator is to render the original as closely as possible into a readable English form. Below we have Irving Lo's version of the poem.

> While drunk, I knew only to laugh and make merry;
> Where's the time to grieve?
> Lately, I've come to know ancient tomes,
> To believe in them was all wrong.
>
> Last night I lay drunk by the pine tree,
> And I asked the pine, "How drunk am I?"
> Half fearing the pine was moving to lift me up,
> With one hand pushing the pine, I said, "Go away."

This, of course, illustrates only one method of translating from Chinese poetry, but although the translations in this volume vary greatly in form and in style, they all adhere to one general guideline: to present the thought content of each poem and also the nuances of words.

While the emphasis of the *K'uei Hsing* venture, and of this volume, is the presentation of hitherto unavailable translations from East and Central Asian literatures, we feel that the short introductions before each selection, generally critical and historical in nature, are necessary. Translations are occasionally followed by a separate set of notes, which include the explanation of literary allusions and references. These allusions, much loved by poets of the Orient, often prove baffling to those not brought up in the traditions of the East.

We hope that this volume will take our readers on a pleasurable journey to the wonderful and strangely hospitable domain of the literatures of the Orient, the realm of our Lord K'uei Hsing.

LIU WU-CHI

K'uei Hsing

A REPOSITORY OF ASIAN LITERATURE IN TRANSLATION

Lu In (Lu Yin)

THE THIRTEEN EXTANT POEMS

TRANSLATED BY HUGH M. STIMSON

INTRODUCTION

DURING the Tarng[1] (T'ang) Dynasty (618–906), a major Chinese poetic form called *shy* (*shih*) developed to its highest point. Among the masters of this form were such giants of Chinese literature as Wang Wei (699–759), Lii Bair (Li Po, 701–62), Duh Fuu (Tu Fu, 712–70), and Bair Jiuyih (Po Chü-i, 772–846). Many excellent translations have made these four poets familiar to Western readers. Recently other poets, especially those who like Bair Jiuyih lived in the latter part of the dynasty, have received careful critical attention in the West, and their works have become familiar in translation. Some of these poets centered around Harn Yuh (Han Yü, 768–824), better known for the part he played in the neo-classical reform of prose essays than for his poetry. Of these at least two will be familiar to Western readers: Menq Jiau (Meng Chiao, 751–814), and Lii Heh (Li Ho, 790–816). A minor poet whose name is associated with Harn Yuh and Menq Jiau is Lu In (Lu Yin, 746–810). As far as I know, none of the thirteen short poems under his name in the *Complete Tarng shy* (*Ch'üan T'ang shih*) ch. 470, which are all that remains of his huge output, have been translated into English. The translations offered here will perhaps show how good a minor Tarng poet can be. I also hope that they will stimulate interest in bringing the works of other little-known poets of the period to the attention of the English-speaking public.

All the biographical data we have on Lu In appear in a funerary inscription written for him by Harn Yuh.[2] This brief notice gives Lu In's home town as Fannyang (Fan-yang), a Tarng commandery whose chief city is the modern Dahshing (Ta-hsing), Herbeei (Hopeh) Province, less than ten kilometers south of the southern boundary of the Beeijing (Peking) municipal district. In his sixty-fifth year he died in Dengfeng Shiann (Teng-feng Hsien), in the modern province of Hernan (Honan) about 40 kilometers due south of the Yellow River and about 60 kilometers southeast of Lohyang (Loyang). He held the minor position of Dengfeng Shiann*wey* (Teng-feng Hsien-*wei*), or Chief of Employees in Dengfeng Shiann. His friends included Menq Jiau, who wrote ten dirges for him. Menq Jiau and other higher-ranking officials succeeded in recommending him for promotion, but he had to decline it on account of illness. A former Prime Minister, Jenq Yuching (Cheng Yü-ch'ing, 746–820), helped support him and at his request paid for his funeral; Harn Yuh himself bought the coffin.

Lu In was buried near Mount Song (Mount Sung, the highest of the Five Sacred Peaks, in Hernan, just north of Dengfeng Shiann) in his first wife's tomb. Sudden death had already deprived him of a son; surviving him were only an unmarried daughter who had become a Buddhist nun, and, presumably, his second wife. Of his intellectual activities, Harn Yuh says that he was a prolific poet and wrote over a thousand pages of verse during his lifetime; also that he was an omnivorous reader, and that what he read he used only to supply content for his poetry.

Here then are the thirteen extant poems of Lu In. They are in the *shy* style, keeping the number of syllables per line constant throughout the poem and using line-end rhymes in even-numbered lines. The first five poems are each eight lines long; there is one rhyme per poem; even-numbered lines rhyme in all five, and in the second poem the first line rhymes as well; the lines are five syllables long with a fixed caesura after the second syllable: 'dum dum, dum dum dum.' The next three poems also use five-syllable lines with the same caesura position, but they are only four lines long; the second and fourth lines rhyme. The last five poems have four seven-syllable lines with two caesuras, one after the second syllable and the other after the fourth: 'dum dum, dum dum, dum dum dum.' In the ninth, tenth, twelfth, and thirteenth poems, the first, second, and fourth lines rhyme; in the eleventh poem only the second and fourth lines rhyme. In translating I have not tried to imitate the rhyme scheme, nor have I invented a way of representing in English the peculiarly Chinese device of regulating tones to produce pleasing variety within the line and antithetical balance between lines of a couplet. But I have always kept the original line order, and in all but the second poem I have managed to preserve the Chinese word order to this extent: Chinese words that follow the last caesura are represented by English words that follow the corresponding caesura in the English line.[3]

THE THIRTEEN EXTANT POEMS OF LU IN

[1] The first poem compares the situation of a lady (or, more precisely, secondary wife) recently arrived in the household of her new master with that of the horse she was traded for. The horse is a good one, from Ferghana, in Central Asia: in power and excellence it is like a dragon. But after all the horse is not really the dragon it resembles; in somewhat the same way, the lady must play a subordinate role with respect to the first wife, the "phoenix" of the first line.

A LADY IN EXCHANGE FOR A HORSE

Companion to a phoenix:
   the lady in the tower;
resembling a dragon:
   the Ferghanan in the stables.
In the same year
   they left their former favors;
in different lands
   accept their new kindness.
The fragrant apartment:
   a place for changing clothes;
a dusty film:
   marks of his snorting grass.
Successive whinnies,
   tears that she will indulge:
they both long
   for their master's gate.

[2] The seventh night of the seventh lunar month is supposed to be the time when two stars, the Ox Leader, or Herdboy, and the Weaving Girl have their yearly rendezvous across the River, or Milky Way, which separates them the rest of the year. The last line of this poem echoes a line in *Chuu tsyr* (*Ch'u tz'u*) "Jeou ge: Shaw sy minq (Chiu ke: Shao szu-ming):" "No sadness is sadder than separation while alive."

SEVENS' NIGHT

When the River is bright and the moon is cool,
the Herdboy and the Weaving Girl meet:
their happiness is exactly then;
a waterclock—whom is it really for?
Surely, they cannot complain that fall speeds by;
all they can do is beg the night to delay.
But it overwhelms the traveler and his wife:
for ten years have they wept, alive but apart.

[3] During the cool nights of early fall, one is still apt to sleep on a mat of finely woven rushes. Such mats are more appropriate to summer: cool air circulating through the mat makes hot nights bearable. The "River" in the third line again refers to the Milky Way. "White elms" as an epithet for stars goes back to an old song: "What is there in the sky? / One by one white elms have been planted."

MOONLIT NIGHT

Dew falls;
   coolness rises from the mat;
no one around;
   moonlight fills the courtyard.
Hard to hear
   are the waves going up the River;
I only gaze
   at stars: white elms.
Around the tree
   goes a magpie: lone percher;
at the window
   flies a glowworm: approaching darkness.
In a moment
   they settle in orchid shadows
and think how together
   they sample various aromas.

[4]

MIDSUMMER
sent to someone south of the Yangtze

The fifth moon
   will soon be here;
but for three years
   the traveler has not returned.
Her dream complete,
   she goes a thousand miles;
from wine awakened,
   there come a hundred sorrows.
In evening dusk,
   at times, she looks at hibiscus;
in her sad pain,
   she does not eat a plum.
Useless, to take
   the round, white fan:
she would go on and send it,
   but then she hesitates.

[5] The *Book of Changes* under "Chyan" (Ch'ien) says, "Clouds follow dragons; the wind follows tigers." It is the essential nature of clouds to be big and billowy, fit to be included in the retinue of a dragon. The *Gongyang juann* (Kung-yang chuan) to "Shi 31" ("Hsi 31") says that on one of the sacred peaks, Mount Tay (T'ai), clouds come out of the mountain, striking rocks. When clouds rake across rocks they disperse in elegantly patterned wisps. "Jade descent" as an epithet for the blue sky appears in a poem by Yang Shyh'eh (Yang Shih-e, fl. 800) entitled "Picnic in a pavilion by the Yangtze" ("Jiangtyng youyann" [Chiang-t'ing yu-yen]), and in the famous "Song of everlasting sorrow" ("Charng henn ge" [Ch'ang hen ke]), by Bair Jiuyih (Po Chü-i). An alternate translation for the fifth and six lines would be: "They make no screen for the light of the crossing moon; / they make indistinct the gleams of the tipping River." "Tipping River" as an epithet for the Milky Way as it tips toward the West as dawn approaches appears in Shieh Hueylian (Hsieh Hui-lien, 397–433), "On Sevens' Night, singing about the Herdboy and the Weaving Girl" ("Chiyeh, yeong Niou-Neu" [Ch'i-ye, yung Niu-Nü]).

CLOUDS ABOUT TO MELT AWAY

They want to hide
   their nature: to follow dragons;
there yet remains
   their elegance, when they strike rocks.
They drift along,
   cling to the jade descent,
by what they seem,
   mistaken for other-than-clouds.
They cross the moon
   but do not screen its light;
they tip toward the River
   and blur its gleams.
If they should chance by
   a place of torrential rain,
they would surely become
   rising, billowing clouds.

[6]

MEETING AN ENVOY TO THE FRONTIER

For years
   no real news;
every night
   she dreams of a frontier city.
Her sleeve covers
   a thousand lines of tears;
a letter encloses
   one foot of feeling.

[7]

MOVING TO ANOTHER RESIDENCE

Since I came
    to live in Western Syhchuan,
only you
    have I parted from with feeling.
Often we met;
    across the street was too far;
but now, between us
    is an entire city.

[8]

AT PERNGKOOU,[4] MEETING A FRIEND

In difficult times
    we have been long apart;
at court and away
    our comradeship grew deep.
Changed
    are the norms of that time;
useless, what remains:
    our heart of former days.

[9]

THE RAIN HAS STOPPED
I climb the north riverbank and send this to a friend

The rice plants are yellow, extend everywhere
    the millet is glossy rich;
amid fields, trees, and successive hills,
    a torrent flows of itself.
I remember back, years ago,
    in the Pyngyih[5] region,
when you, Master Shieh, escorted me
    up to the top of a tower.

[10] During the poet's lifetime there was trouble with foreign nations at China's borders. Eastern Turks at the north of the present province of Shanshi (Shansi, an area known to ancient geographers as Bingjou, Ping-chou) made military garrisons there necessary. In times of particular stress, able-bodied civilians would be expected to put aside frivolous undertakings, such as might be associated with the ancient southern state of Chuu (Ch'u), and adopt the more military bearing of another ancient southern state, Wu: "Hook of Wu" in the first line is a sickle-shaped weapon.

FRIENDS AND RELATIONS IN CHARNG'AN

No Chuu orchids at my belt;
    at my belt a Hook of Wu;
I bring wine to the main city gate
    and part from an old comrade.
My years of age are many now,
    but the muscle is still there;
I'll take my bow and arrow
    and go as far as Bingjou.

[11] The Chinese year is divided into twenty-four periods according to the position of the sun in the zodiac. "White Dew" is the name of one of these periods, ending with the autumnal equinox. Migrating wild geese serve as a link between separated loved ones; chirping cicadas exacerbate the pain of loneliness. The weather has turned chilly; one is reminded of winter; it is meaningless to carry a fan.

SAD AT AUTUMN

Wild geese cross the autumn emptiness;
    the blue sky is far;
cicadas chirp in sparse-growing trees;
    the White Dew is wintry.
By the steps, wilting orchids
    still have some spirit;
in her hand, the round fan
    has gradually lost its point.

[12]
EVENING CICADA

Hidden deep in a tall willow,
 its back to the slanting rays,
it has power to rouse his lonely sadness
 and to lessen his former girth.
And yet it fears that the traveler
 will not become white-headed;
again and again it changes trees,
 making its noise as it flies.

[13] Weiyang (Wei-yang) Commandery, an archaic name for a large area in southeastern China, serves to designate the city in that area later known as Yangjou (Yang-chou) in Jiangsu (Kiangsu) Province. In the Tarng Dynasty Yangjou was famous for its opulence and for the variety of its entertainments. Many of its beautiful women, with skin like white jade, must have gravitated there from outlying farm areas.

AT A PAVILION TO THE WEST
 of Weiyang Commandery: to a friend

Duckweed swishes on the windy pond;
 its fragrance fills the boat;
willow leaves are in quiet array
 against the late spring sky.
The Jade One's present-day
 matters of the heart:
how are they like when she rode a goat,
 those years, going to market?

NOTES

1. In transcribing Chinese names and terms I prefer a romanization that indicates the tones. The one that does this with the least typographical difficulty is the National Romanization, where letters represent the tones in an intricate but systematic and, ultimately, memorable way. Of course, using this romanization will help only those who have learned enough Chinese to know what the four tones are and who have exposed themselves to National Romanization itself. To others, accustomed to the Wade transcription and to postal spellings of place names, having this romanization foisted upon them will at the very least be a nuisance, or, worse, a source of genuine confusion. To avoid this possibility of confusion, I have indicated the alternative romanization in parenthesis following the Chinese word at its first occurrence, except in the poems. In poem 7, line 2, alternate romanization is Szechwan.

2. "Dengfeng Shiannwey Lu-In muhjyh" (Teng-feng Hsien-wei Lu Yin mu-chich), in Maa-Tongbor (Ma T'ung-po), *Harn-Changli wen jyi jiawjuh* (*Han Ch'ang-li wen chi chiao-chu*), p. 211 (Shanqhae [Shanghai], 1957).

3. My friend and colleague, Professor T. Y. Li, went over these translations in an earlier version, and his generous help is hereby gratefully acknowledged.

4. Perngkoou (P'eng-k'ou) is in the northwest of the present Perng Shiann (P'eng Hsien), Syhchuan (Szechwan) Province, about forty kilometers north-northwest of Cherngdu (Ch'eng-tu).

5. Pyngyih (P'ing-i) is now called Dahlih (Ta-li), and is in Shaanshi (Shensi) Province on the Loh (Lo) River, about one hundred ten kilometers northeast of the Tarng capital city, Charng-an (Ch'ang-an).

Ssu-ma Kuang

INSTRUCTIONS ON FRUGALITY FOR MY SON K'ANG

TRANSLATED BY A. W. SARITI

INTRODUCTION

SSU-MA KUANG was one of the outstanding scholar-officials of his time. His most valuable contribution was in the field of history. The monumental *Tzu Chih T'ung Chien* (Comprehensive Mirror for Aid in Government), which he compiled on imperial order between 1067 and 1084, is a general history of China from 403 B.C. to 959 A.D. Because this work is a compilation of source materials rather than an interpretive narration, it is of special value to the modern-day historian. For Ssu-ma, the facts of history were plain and provided a mirror of men's actions that could aid those who sought to govern. There was no need, then, to "interpret"—the facts spoke for themselves. Such scholarly objectivity, albeit unwittingly come by, was unfortunately not applied to a later abridgment of this work, the *T'ung Chien Kang Mu* (General Outline of the Comprehensive Mirror) by the famous Sung Neo-Confucian philosopher, Chu Hsi. It was this book, translated by Father de Mailla under the title *Histoire Générale de la Chine* and published in the 1780's, that became the general fund for information on China available to the West.

In the field of political science and moral philosophy (difficult to separate in traditional China) Ssu-ma made no lasting achievement. Considering himself a model Confucian, he sought to meet the new political and economic challenges, which threatened to topple the Sung dynasty, with an old prescription—an emphasis on orthodox Confucian values. The intervening years from the time of Confucius (551–479 B.C.) to the Sung had brought many changes, and Ssu-ma Kuang's narrow interpretation of the traditional value system proved useless in the face of the new problems that confronted eleventh-century China. The leading force for reform in Sung China was Wang An-shih (who also considered himself a model Confucian).

His broader interpretation of the Confucian tradition allowed him to propose bolder solutions to these problems. His proposals, however, owing both to the strong opposition headed by Ssu-ma Kuang and the questionable quality of the reform administrators, never received a full and fair opportunity. They also ended in failure.

One of the more pressing problems of the Sung was the dwindling state finances. This situation could be met in several ways. The government could attempt to stimulate the economy, it could raise new revenue by taxation, or it could cut its own expenses. Ssu-ma Kuang favored "fiscal responsibility"—government frugality. The Confucian concept of frugality was applicable to the state as well as to the individual. There were, of course, other perhaps baser motives for Ssu-ma's position (e.g., he was a representative of the landed gentry). Nevertheless, within the context of traditional Confucian philosophy, he was able to construct a tenable position. The world had from the beginning, Ssu-ma had once noted, a limited, finite number of goods; only man himself was continually increasing. Rather than equally distributing what was available, the government should seek to make men satisfied with their station in life (*an fen*). Rather than "seek profit," men and government should conserve what they have. Ssu-ma, in the following advice to his son, outlines this position on frugality.

The source for my translation is "Hsün Chien Shih K'ang," *Wen-kuo Wen-cheng Ssu-ma Kuang Wen-chi* (*Ssu Pu Ts'ung K'an* ed.), 69: 505–506.

SSU-MA KUANG / INSTRUCTIONS ON FRUGALITY FOR MY SON K'ANG

I AM descended from a poor family which from generation to generation has inherited an unsullied reputation.[1] By nature I find no pleasure in showy extravagance. When I was a small child, my elders put costly and elegant clothes on me and I, embarrassed by this uncalled-for extravagance, threw them off. At the age of twenty I won honors at the examinations,[2] but at the celebration fete given for all the successful candidates I was the only one who did not wear flowers on his head. My fellow graduates said to me: "Gifts of the sovereign cannot be refused." And so I stuck a bloom in my hair. All my life I have taken just enough food to satisfy my hunger, just enough clothes to shelter myself from the cold. Yet I did not venture to wear tattered and filthy clothes thereby seeking fame through breaching custom. But this was all merely following my nature, nothing more.

The multitude glorifies wasteful extravagance while I alone, led on by my moral nature, consider temperate simplicity a thing of beauty. People laugh at me and say that I am mean and crude, but I don't let this distress me. I answer them saying, "Confucius has said: 'It is better to be mean than to be insubordinate' and 'The cautious seldom err' and also 'A knight whose heart is set upon the Way, but who is ashamed of wearing shabby clothes and eating coarse food, is not worth calling into counsel'."[3] The ancients considered frugality a superior virtue, but people today look upon it as something of which one should be ashamed. Alas! how strange this is!

In recent years customs have been especially extravagant, with messengers dressing like scholars and farmers wearing silken shoes. I remember when the late duke, my father, was Prefect's Administrator during the T'ien-sheng era. When guests arrived the wine was always set out, and three or five—never more than seven—toasts were made. The wine they drank had been bought in the marketplace, and the fruits were no more than might ordinarily be expected: pears, chestnuts, dates, persimmons. Minced meat and vegetable broth were the only delicacies, and the table utensils were porcelain and lacquer ware. At that time such was the custom in all the gentry families—people did not criticize each other on this account. Although material things might not have been in abundant supply, yet there was a sincere spirit of friendliness that pervaded all. These gatherings were frequent and the etiquette demanded of such occasions was diligently followed. But today, well, if the wine is not "palace made," the fruit and delicacies not rare imports from some distant clime, if there are not numerous varieties of food or if the table is not brimming with dinnerware, why then these gentry families do not dare receive guests. They often spend months in preparation before they dare to send out the invitations. Indeed, if such is not the case people are quick to criticize and suppose the guilty party quite niggardly. Thus, those who do not fall in with the customary extravagance are few indeed! Alas! customs have degenerated to this point. Although it is true that those in office have no power to prohibit these customs, can they bear to help them along?

I have heard that formerly, when Duke Li Wen-ching was prime minister, he built a home inside the city gate, and that the reception room was barely large enough for a horse to turn around in. Someone said that it was too small, and the duke, laughing, answered, "A private home is to be handed down to one's posterity. If this were to be a prime minister's reception room then certainly it would be too small. If, however, it is to serve as a room in which one may offer sacrifices to his ancestors, then it is quite large enough indeed."

Once, when Duke Lu was censor, Emperor Chen-tsung sent out a messenger with an urgent summons for him. The messenger found Lu in a wineshop, and when the duke arrived at court the emperor asked him whence he came. Duke Lu answered truthfully, whereupon the emperor asked, "My dear minister, you hold a noble and much-respected office. How is it that you were drinking at a wineshop?" Lu answered, "Your minister's home is a poor one. There is no tableware, nor are there fine delicacies or fruits, thus when guests arrive I take them to a wineshop for entertainment." The emperor, impressed by this frankness, gained a new respect for the duke.

Chang Wen-chieh, as prime minister, supported himself in the same manner as he had when he served as secretary in Ho Yang. One of his close relatives reproved him, saying, "The duke now receives a large salary, yet he continues to support himself in this manner. Although the duke may believe he is being frugal and is of pure character, some people who don't know him better feel that he is merely pretending humility, like the famous Kung-sun with his cotton garments. The duke should not let himself seem so much like the masses."

Chang sighed and replied, "Although my present salary could certainly permit my whole family to live quite luxuriously, how could I be sure that some calamity would not occur? You see, it is a fact of man's natural disposition that to proceed from frugality to luxury is easy, while to regress from luxury to frugality is difficult. How can one suppose that my salary will always remain at the present level? If my salary suddenly became different from what it is today my family, had it been long accustomed to a life of luxury, would not be able to make the abrupt change from luxury to frugality. This would certainly lead to the ruin of the family. How does this compare with a situation in which, regardless of my official position or even whether I am alive or dead, they live always together as they do today." Ah! such a thoughtful and farseeing worthy! How can any ordinary man hope to arrive at such heights?

Yü-sun has said, "Frugality is the universal virtue, extravagance the great evil." This means that all those who possess virtue have come by way of frugality. Now, if one is frugal he has few desires. If the Superior Man has few desires, then he is not a slave to material things and can follow the way of orthodox principles. If the Mean Man has few desires, then he can be cautious about his person and sparing in his use of resources, thus keeping criminal offense at a distance and making his family prosper. Thus it is said, "Frugality is the universal virtue." On the other hand, if one is extravagant he has many desires. If the Superior Man has many desires, then he covets wealth, longs for honor and by his perverted principles invites calamity. If the Mean Man has many desires, then he seeks after many things, uses his resources recklessly, ruins his family and destroys himself. For this reason, if the Mean Man holds a position in the government he is certain to be corrupt, if he has no position in government he is certain to be criminal. Thus it is said, "Extravagance is the great evil."

Formerly Cheng K'au-fu [an ancestor of Confucius] subsisted only on thick gruel. Meng Hsi-tzu knew from this that Cheng's posterity would certainly include a great man.

Chi Wen-tzu was Prime Minister to three sovereigns, yet when he died his concubines wore no silk at the funeral nor did his horses eat grain. The sovereign considered this a mark of Chi's loyalty.[4]

Kuan Chung used engraved *kuei* [a kind of vessel used either to contain delicacies or for the purpose of holding sacrificial offerings] and wore crimson chin straps to hold his official hat in place. He "carved hills on the pillars and duckweed on the joists"—he was very extravagant, and Confucius despised him for his smallness.

When Kung-shu Wen-tzu entertained Duke Ling of Wei, Shih Ch'iu knew that calamity would follow, for Kung-shu was rich and the duke covetous. But Kung-shu was an exception; he was rich without being proud. This was not the case with his son, Shu. When Shu became head of the household, a charge was consequently trumped up against him because of his wealth, and he was forced to flee.[5]

Ho Tseng daily consumed ten thousand cash worth of food, and his grandson, when he became head of the family, led the family to ruin through his unbounded pride.

Shih Ch'ung made a great show of his wasteful extravagance to impress people, and it was because of this that he finally died at the executioner's hand.

In more recent times the extravagance and gaiety of Duke K'ou-lai was unsurpassed for a time. Nevertheless, because of his great achievements there was no one who criticized him. Today, however, his family, once accustomed to a life of luxury, is without resources and in poverty.

There are indeed many examples of those who through frugality have established themselves and through extravagance destroyed themselves. I cannot relate them all here in detail but have rather chosen to select several men by whose example you may be instructed. You should not only apply this lesson to yourself but should use it to instruct your descendants so that they may know the mores of their predecessors.

NOTES

1. i.e., has not engaged in an occupation reckoned dishonorable.
2. Kuang won first honors at the *Chin Shih* examinations.
3. The translation of the final saying is from Arthur Waley, *Analects of Confucius* (New York: Random House, Inc., 1938), pp. 103–104.
4. See *Tso Chuan*, Duke Hsiang, 5th Year: "He acted as chief minister to three dukes, and yet had accumulated nothing for himself—is he not to be pronounced loyal?"
5. See *Tso Chuan*, Duke Ting, 13th Year.

Hsiang Hsiu

FU ON REMEMBERING THE PAST

TRANSLATED BY ROGER BAILEY

INTRODUCTION

HSIANG HSIU, whose *tzu* or style name was Tzu-ch'i, was a member of the famous third-century literary coterie known as the Seven Sages of the Bamboo Grove. He is known primarily as a great scholar and commentator of the *Chuang-tzu Book;* Chuang-tzu (369?–286? B.C.) was a famous writer and Taoist philosopher. Little of Hsiang's purely literary work has survived. Hsi K'ang, whom he eulogizes in his *"Fu* on Remembering the Past," was a fellow member of the Seven Sages and a most celebrated performer on the lute. Hsi K'ang wrote the long *"Fu* on the Lute," his best-known work, which was translated into English by R. H. Van Gulik (*Hsi K'ang and His Poetical Essay on the Lute*, Tokyo, 1941); he also wrote some miscellaneous lyric poems, and his self-revelatory "Letter to Shan T'ao" has been translated, with minor omissions, by Professor James R. Hightower (in Cyril Birch, ed., *Anthology of Chinese Literature from Early Times to the Fourteenth Century,* New York, 1965). The outstanding poet of the Seven Sages was Jüan Chi (210–263); many of his *Poems from my Heart* are in English versions.

These men lived during the Three Kingdoms period (221–264 A.D.) when the Ssu-ma family was trying to establish its legitimacy as the ruling house of China. Jüan Chi's alternative to distasteful submission to a usurper was to escape into grotesque unconventionality. Hsi K'ang was unable to avoid running afoul of the authorities and was executed. His death seems to have broken Hsiang Hsiu's capacity for resistance: he was on his way to assuming an office when he wrote this poem.

Written in alternating prose and verse, the *fu*, which flourished in the Han dynasty, was largely descriptive in nature. The immense length and obscure magnificence which often characterize this form undoubtedly were appropriate to the celebration of the glories of the Han dynasty. Like other later *fu,* however, Hsiang Hsiu's "*Fu* on Remembering the Past" was obviously written in obedience to a genuinely lyrical impulse.

The original text for my translation is in the *Wen Hsüan, chüan* 16.

HSIANG HSIU/FU ON REMEMBERING THE PAST

I USED to live near Hsi K'ang and Lü An; they were both men of untrammeled genius. But Hsi had high and unrestrained aspirations and Lü had a liberal and daring mind, and afterwards, for one reason or another, they were both executed. Hsi's artistic gift was all-embracing, and he was particularly skilled with string and wind instruments. Just before he was to die, he turned to look at the shadows caused by the sun; then he asked for a lute and played on it. Having made a journey to the west, I returned and passed by his old hut. At that time, the sun was sinking below the horizon, and it was cold and bitter. A neighbor was playing the flute, and its solitary sound carried far. When I thought back on the joys of our former association, I was moved to sigh aloud; therefore, I composed this *Fu*:

> I had been ordered to go to the distant capital;
> Afterwards, I turned around and traveled back to the north.
> I crossed the Yellow River by boat
> And passed by the old dwelling in Shanyang.
> Gazing on the bleak and desolate wilderness,
> I halted my carriage at a corner of the city wall,
> And following in the very footsteps of my two friends,
> I passed by the empty hut in the secluded lane.
> I sighed, remembering the "Hanging Millet" and its lament for the House of Chou;
> I grieved, remembering the "Wheat Grain" poet as he passed through the Wastes of Yin.
> Recalling the past made me long for my friends,
> And I faltered, my heart irresolute.
> The beams and roof still stand unharmed,
> But where have the spirits and shapes of my friends gone?
> Of old, when Li Ssu was about to be executed,
> He sighed long for his yellow dog:
> I mourn that when Master Hsi took his eternal departure,
> He looked back at the shadows from the sun and played a lute.
> Fully knowing what his fate was to be,
> He occupied himself even in those last few moments of his life.

I heard the mournful sound of the flute,
Its lovely strains now cut off and now continuing.
Since my carriage was about to set out,
I raised my brush and wrote what was in my heart.

NOTES

line 4   Shanyang is in present-day Honan Province.
lines 9 and 10   The "Hanging Millet" is poem No. 65 in *The Classic of Poetry*, an anthology of Chinese poetry compiled mainly during the Chou dynasty. The "Wheat Grain" poet was Chi-tzu of the Yin Dynasty, which preceded the Chou. After the fall of Yin, Chi-tzu passed by its ruined palaces and wastelands; greatly moved, he composed the song, "Wheat Grain."
line 15   Li Ssu was a minister to the first emperor of the Ch'in dynasty who helped to establish the Ch'in empire.

Hsin Ch'i-chi

THIRTY LYRICS BY "A POET'S POET"

TRANSLATED BY IRVING YUCHENG LO

INTRODUCTION

THE development of poetic genres within a single but manifold tradition often shows a pattern of rapid growth followed by a decline. Just when the sap of creative energy is about to run dry, a new genius whose gift for language is equal to the task is once again able to chart a new course for poetry's continuous development. Hsin Ch'i-chi (1140–1207) initiated one of these major resurgences with his lyric poems, called *tz'u*, a subgenre of Chinese poetry.

Hsin wrote at the beginning of the Southern Sung dynasty, but his works were so voluminous—over 600 poems[1]—that not all aspects of his style have been recognized by critics or even by his most ardent admirers. His work had been almost totally ignored by Western readers, except for a few of his shorter poems, until some of his more serious compositions were included in recent histories and anthologies of Chinese literature.[2] This introduction to Hsin's art, through my own translation of thirty of his poems, attempts to illustrate the range and diversity of his style as a lyricist. But to assess Hsin's achievements properly, I must first sketch a summary of his life[3] and give a brief account of the development of lyric poetry from its emergence toward the end of the T'ang dynasty (618–907).

Among the subgenres of Chinese poetry, or *shih* (a word also used to mean poetry in its collective sense), the most widely translated and most popularly known in the West are the quatrains (*chüeh-chü*) and "regulated poetry" (*lü-shih*), consisting of either five or seven words for each line, written according to strict prosodic schemes. This type of poetry, which reached the height of its development in the middle of the eighth century, has become known exclusively as the "new style poetry" (*chin-t'i shih*) in contradistinction to the "ancient-style poetry" (*ku-t'i shih*). The latter refers to poems of indeterminate length, also popular with T'ang poets, which require a less rigid adherence to the prosodic scheme and permit the occasional use of some shorter or longer lines, while maintaining a predominantly five- or seven-word line. *Shih* as a form of poetry continued to be written by Sung poets, and Sung *shih* is still much admired.[4] But immediately after the T'ang dynasty, during the Five Dynasties period (907–960), as well as the Northern Sung (960–1126) and the Southern Sung (1127–1279) dynasties, a new form, the *tz'u*, engaged the attention of many poets.

The *tz'u* poem was originally written to music, following the prosodic "pattern" (*tiao*) of each tune-title. It was usually not given another title to indicate its subject matter. Sometimes rendered into English as "song-poem,"[5] *tz'u* is essentially characterized by flexibility and irregularity in arrangement. Hence it is also known in Chinese by another name—the "long-and-short verses" (*ch'ang-tuan chü*).[6] Each poem may consist of as few as fourteen words or as many as 240 (as in the "*Ying-t'i-hsu*" tune), depending on the tune-title. Lines may vary in length but rarely exceed eight or nine words for the longest lines among the more widely-used tunes. During the Southern Sung period, the longer tunes (*ch'ang-tiao*) became more popular. Their musical origin was by then forgotten, and subject-titles were more commonly given. *Tz'u* emerged as an important genre and the medium of a more personal kind of poetry—as intimately revealing of the poet's life and thought as was Tu Fu's poetry (*shih*) approximately four centuries earlier.

Over 200 years had elapsed between the appearance of the first *tz'u* anthology, the *Hua-chien chi* (Among-the-Flowers Collection, preface dated 940), and the time Hsin Ch'i-chi wrote his lyrics. The proliferation of both tune-titles[7] and poems had proceeded so rapidly during this time that a complete collection of the Sung lyrics (*Ch'üan-Sung tz'u*), culled from earlier anthologies and individual works, records close to 20,000 lyrics written by over 1,330 poets.[8] Yet despite the great number of *tz'u*, many individual poets wrote within rather narrow ranges of both subject matter and style. With the possible exception of Su Tung-p'o (1037–1101), each lyricist usually achieved one distinctive voice and did not experiment outside of it. But while Hsin Ch'i-chi is generally admired, along with Su Tung-p'o, for his vigorous and unrestrained style, he is also recognized—and sometimes censured—for his wide use of allusions; a sobriquet often hurled at him was "bookbag-thrower" (*tiao-shu-tai*).[9]

Chinese critics often disagree as to who the four most important *tz'u* poets of the two Sung eras are.[10] This difference of opinion notwithstanding, Hsin's name occurs on practically every list. Moreover, the lyrics of the Southern Sung do not lose any vigor when compared with those of the earlier era. As a seventeenth-century critic put it, "whereas T'ang poetry deteriorated with its three successive changes of style . . . the *tz'u* poetry since the establishment of the Southern Sung in 1127 could not be spoken of as belonging to a 'middle' or 'late' period in its development."[11] To put it another way, Hsin Ch'i-chi might be considered as an inheritor of all that had been written up to his time: he alone met the challenge and realized the full potential of this type of verse; he alone dealt with all kinds of meters and themes, always rejecting the artificial and spurious, always imbuing the *tz'u* with his own voice; and he, among all the major *tz'u* poets, achieved the greatest diversity in style.

Hsin's reputation today appears unassailable both on mainland China and in Taiwan; within the last decade a number of critical and biographical studies of the poet were published in Peking and Taipei.[12] One example of the universal appeal and timeless quality of Hsin's poems is Hu Shih's judgment that Hsin ranked as "the first among major *tz'u* poets."[13] This high critical praise is not without irony since Hu Shih (1891–1962) had been the most vociferous denouncer of the use of allusions (for allusions' sake) during the New Culture Movement in the twenties.

Hsin Ch'i-chi, whose style name was Chia-hsüan,[14] was born only thirteen years after the last two emperors of the Northern Sung had been captured by the Jurchëd, who founded the Chin dynasty in the north of China; the Southern Sung, its capital removed to Lin-an (modern Hangchow), survived for 153 years through a period marked by an uneasy peace, military defeats, and humiliating truce settlements. Hsin's birthplace was Li-ch'eng (modern Tsinan) in Shantung, and he spent his boyhood years in the north. The details of those years are rather obscure; he was said to have studied under a famous scholar[15] and to be known as a classmate of Tang Huai-ying (1134–1211),[16] who later became a literary luminary and high official in the Chin court. He was reported to have undertaken two journeys as far north as Yen-shan (modern Ta-hsing *hsien* in Hopei); according to one historical source, he passed the *chin-shih* examination,[17] a detail not mentioned in his biography in the Sung history *(Sung-shih)*.[18]

In 1162, the poet moved south and burst upon the scene at the court of the Southern Sung. He joined a leader of the anti-Jurchëd uprisings and in two separate episodes (one of which will be described in the notes to Poem A3) won admiration for his physical courage and intense loyalty. Yet these acts of patriotism earned him the appointment as only a minor official of the lower eighth rank, as junior secretary (*ch'eng-wu-lang*) and later as a signatory official (*ch'ien-p'an*) on the prefectural staff of Chiang-ying in Kiangsu. During the next eight years (1162–1170) a policy of appeasement continued to be favored by Emperor Hsiao-tsung, and the poet advanced very little in his political career. During this period he presented the ten memorials to the throne entitled "The Humble Offerings of Ten Discourses" (*Mei-ch'in shih-lun*); in these he outlined his plan for the reconquest of the lost territory. Another set of "Nine Discourses" (*Chiu-i*), which he wrote at this time for the Chief Councilor of State Yü Yün-wen (1110–1174), dealt with military strategy and fiscal reform. In 1170 the poet was given his second audience with the emperor.

Hsin spent the next dozen years or so as a tireless administrator in various parts of south-central China, as Assistant Fiscal Intendant (*chuan-yün fu-shih*) or as Judicial Intendant (*t'i-tien hsing-yü*) in Anhwei, Kiangsi, Hunan, and Hupeh. Although rising no higher than the sixth rank as Lord Assistant Chief Justice (*ta-li shao-ch'ing*) and also as Compiler at the Imperial Archive (*pi-ko hsiu-chuan*), Hsin became a controversial figure in politics by espousing and carrying out bold and innovative policies. These included the successful suppression of rebellions, the undertaking of construction projects or famine relief work, and the most controversial of all, the organization of a large militia force in Hunan against an imperial edict.

In 1181 unfavorable criticism forced him to retire to Ch'ien-shan, near Shang-jao, in Kiangsi, where he built a villa by a scenic lake called Tai-hu (Ribbon Lake). There he took on the style name of the "Hermit of Farming Pavilion" (*Chia-hsüan chü-shih*), or simply Chia-hsüan. He remained at his beloved villa for nearly two decades until the time of his death, except for three years (1191–1194) when he served as Pacification Administrator (*an-fu-shih*) of Fukien, where he was again abruptly removed when an imperial censor accused him of "spending money like dirt and sand and killing people without any hesitation."[19]

Hsin Ch'i-chi's checkered career is extraordinary for a Chinese poet. Since the time of the Three Kingdoms (220–280), few poets in China had shown any talent for military affairs, although there had been a few generals who wrote one or two good poems. Hsin's youthful exploits together with his many acts of generosity and courage in his later life all evince the spirit of the ancient Chinese knight-errantry (known as *hsieh* or *hsia*) and show a remarkable affinity with the ideals and the career of Li Po.[20]

His loyalty to the emperor, his selfless dedication to public service, and his broad sympathy with the suffering people—and, of course, his poetic craftsmanship and erudition—also reflect the life-long ideals and ambitions, and achievements, of Tu Fu, China's greatest poet. The distressing events of his time caused by the Jurchëd invasion are certainly comparable to the upheavals brought about by the An Lu-shan Rebellion which Tu Fu witnessed. One might even speculate that Tu Fu would have worked toward similar political and social accomplishments had he been given positions of responsibility under the T'ang government. But Hsin drew his inspiration chiefly from China's exiled poets. The lives of the ancient poets Ch'ü Yüan (died 278 B.C.) and especially T'ao Ch'ien (365–427) whom he affectionately addressed as "my teacher" in one of his poems[21] provided a pattern for the man who was so often misunderstood by his contemporaries. A recent unpublished study of the use of allusions to past literary works (*chi*) in Hsin's poetry shows that although Tu Fu was most often recalled (143 allusions), T'ao Ch'ien (76 allusions) and *Ch'u Tz'u*, the work attributed to Ch'ü Yüan and his followers (71 allusions) were significantly important in his work.[22] Like his poetry his life has many facets; it mirrors a perfect fusion of the Confucian ideal of humanity and this-worldliness with the Taoist ideal of artless spontaneity.

The thirty poems which I have translated here are arranged in groups representing six different styles of the poet. I have numbered the lines according to the original for ease of reference; capitalization is used to begin each of the "long" or "short" lines, and omitted in the case of run-on lines when they are needed to accommodate the longer lines of the original. No rhyme is used.

Group A consists of four of Hsin's most widely appreciated *tz'u*. They typify the patriotic mode of thought and feeling and were written in the unrestrained (*hao-fang*) style akin to that of Su Tung-p'o. These intensely personal poems can be dated on both internal and external evidence with greater certainty than some of Hsin's others since the subject matter is clearly autobiographical (Poems A2 and A3 especially). Poems A1 and A4 are among Hsin's earliest and latest poems respectively; "visiting an ancient site" is a theme widely used by Chinese poets to express their innermost personal thoughts.

The four poems in Group B show by contrast the quality of voluptuous seductiveness (*yen-li*) which is generally considered the hallmark of the *Hua-chien* style. This special kind of poetry, also referred to as the "palace style," had been popularized in an earlier *shih* anthology, the *Yü-t'ai hsin-yung* (New Songs of the Jade Pavilion) from the sixth century. Of course the theme of the boudoir lament appeared still earlier, but after the appearance of the *Hua-chien chi* it became almost exclusively identified with *tz'u* poetry. Another common theme of lyric poetry, of which B2 is an example, became increasingly popular toward the end of the Southern Sung; it belongs to the category known as "purely descriptive (of) things" (*yung-wu*) for which the subject, usually rather narrow, has been preselected, somewhat in the manner of the "rhymeprose" (*fu*) compositions of Han era. Hsin wrote very few of these poems, but even here, within the restrictions of such a narrow topic, the poet has achieved by means of personification a closely-knit structure, which is all the more remarkable when one considers the length of the poem (102 words).

The six poems in Group C reveal Hsin's genius for taking the themes most commonly used by *tz'u* poets of the past and imbuing them with fresh meaning and vigor. The poet writes of grief at parting (C1 and C5), frustration of either political (C2) or romantic aspirations (C3), or laments on the transitoriness of time and youth (C4 and C6). Yet Hsin has successfully amalgamated nearly all the best styles of earlier *tz'u* poets through a variety of poetic means. He achieves this at times through the selective use of allusion, as in C2 where remarkably he builds the poem around a single set of allusions. He also uses analogy (C1 and C3) and variation and repetition (C4), where the word for spring (*ch'un*) is used four times, the word for wind (*feng*) twice, the word for flower (*hua*) twice, and the word *jen* (translated as "people" and "the loved one") twice. In Poem C5 the mood of late spring is rendered through a human situation, that of a woman despairing of her love; whereas in Poem C6 the poet conveys a complex human emotion, a mixture of joy and grief, by means of a detailed cataloguing of spring scenery, including oranges and leeks. In all these poems, the poet's contemplation of the outer world is so intense, his description so vivid, the texture so compact that the poet's own voice is clearly heard. In other words, the commonplace themes of *tz'u* poetry become in Hsin's hands an expression of his own intimate emotions.

Group D introduces seven poems, all of which were written in the simplest style imaginable, reminiscent of the best lines of Po Chü-i, or of T'ao Ch'ien, or of some of the quatrains (*chüeh-chü*) of Tu Fu.

No allusion is used, only very ordinary words, and often colloquialisms which another poet from Hsin's birthplace, Li Ch'ing-chao (1081–1141), was also fond of using in some of her best-remembered *tz'u* poems. Hsin in these sketches of a rustic scene or a simple human situation achieved the unadorned, dispassionate quality that is most prized, but seldom achieved, by Chinese poets. Often described by the critical term *"p'ing-tan,"* which denotes a quality that never cloys or sates, this style of complete artlessness or utter simplicity creates an esthetic effect comparable to the best of Sung monochrome paintings done in the style of *pai-miao* (white or unadorned sketching). This group of Hsin's verses is perhaps the most appealing, and accessible, to Western readers; yet behind the deceptive simplicity there is always a marvelous control of details, a sense of structure, which has made these poems easy to render, but difficult to translate well.

The seven poems in Group E combine plain style with a jocular vein. Poem E5 employs numerous colloquialisms, some bordering on the *risqué*. A favorite tune-title in his humorous light verse is "The Ugly Slave," in which a line in the middle of each stanza is repeated so that the same line must relate to both the preceding and following lines. Poem E7 uses a tune-title from the *Hua-chien chi*, generally known as "Ho-ch'uan," or "Singing by the River"; but Hsin alone chose to preface these two words in the title with the word "T'ang" (dynasty), possibly to indicate his knowledge of the origin of the tune.[23] Poem E7, "Written in Imitation of the *Hua-chien* Style," is clearly a satirical piece, somewhat like Shakespeare's Sonnet 130, in which the conceits of the Elizabethan sonneteering convention are so effectively satirized:

> My mistress' eyes are nothing like the sun;
> Coral is far more red than her lips' red;
> If snow be white, why then her breasts are dun....

A poem that combines humor with erudition (E6) serves as a transition to the last group of poems. Like Poem E6 (114 words in the original), Hsin's more allusive poems, which I have grouped in F, generally use some of the longest tune-titles in the language—the tune-title "*Shao-pien*" (F2), for instance, being the fourth longest of all *tz'u* patterns (203 words). His erudition and his ability to make it relevant to poetry are given ample scope here. Of course, to a greater or lesser degree, the use of allusions had been a common practice among Chinese poets for a long time. Before allusions became stereotyped, they could and did play an integral part in the total meaning of a poem. They function somewhat like the allusions to Greek or Roman mythology in English poetry or, as I have attempted to show elsewhere, nearly in the same manner in which modern poets like T. S. Eliot and David Jones have made use of footnotes to add to the "evocative" power of poetry.[24]

In Hsin's allusive lyrics, however, there is still another innovative feature. He quotes, sometimes *verbatim*, sometimes in adaptations, passages of prose from *The Analects* of Confucius, or *The Book of Mencius*, or the works of other philosophers. Most widely borrowed is the more poetic prose of the *Chuang-tzu* (it alone provides eighty-seven quotations or allusions).[25] In these poems, Hsin is also fond of using many exclamatory or interrogative particles like *yi, tsai* or *hu*, along with other "empty-words" (*hsü-tzu*), or particles, in order to achieve a smooth transition or for the sake of emphasis. As a result, the natural rhythm of the language, aided by the melodic pattern and the use of rhyme, becomes so vitalized as to give birth to a new type of poetry, a kind of metaphysical verse. It is not without cause that Hsin has been sometimes labeled a writer of "*tz'u-lun*," or "lyric discourses," as well as a "bookbag-thrower."

An equally erudite poet of another era, Han Yü (768–824), practiced a similar kind of verbal gymnastics through the use of particles and archaic diction in the five- or seven-word poetry (*shih*) written in the "ancient" style. But the smoothness and the coherence of Hsin's metaphysical lyrics stand in sharp contrast to Han Yü's more rugged lines. This successful fusion of poetry and prose, which was not possible in Han Yü's time, appears to have demonstrated beyond any doubt the malleability and suppleness of *tz'u* as a medium of poetry in contrast to the prosodic rigidity of the *shih*.

These thirty poems by Hsin Ch'i-chi illustrate the full range of Hsin's styles as a lyricist. Forgetting for the moment the traditional terminologies of Chinese literary criticism, one can say that Hsin's poetry is sometimes simple, sometimes sensuous, sometimes passionate —and, of course, on occasion also erudite. He seems just as aware of the important differences between poetry and prose as Milton was in his tract "Of Education." The English poet enumerates the three qualities as essential to the "sublime art" of poetry, and also attempts to distinguish poetry from what he called "the useful Logic" and "the graceful and ornate Rhetoric." To both of these, he wrote, poetry "must be made subsequent, or indeed rather precedent, as being less subtle and fine, but more simple, sensuous, and passionate."[26]

The allusive quality of Hsin's verses is certainly derived from his deep attachment to the philosophers and the classics—China's equivalent of Plato, Aristotle, or Longinus. Despite its origin in music, the rather narrow range of *tz'u* poetry became in the hands of Hsin Ch'i-chi so supple an instrument that he could sum up the best styles of all the great poets of the past—not only T'ao Ch'ien and Tu Fu, but also *Ch'u Tz'u* and *Shih Ching* (Book of Songs)[27]—and at the same time fuse poetry with philosophy into a highly individualized form of art.

Hsin was as steeped in China's ancient traditions as Edmund Spenser was familiar with Greek pastorals and Vergilian eclogues; he was as much in tune with the new poetry of his day as Spenser was with the new influences of Petrarch or the French Pléiade. Both were equally involved in the political tensions of their times: Hsin Ch'i-chi's life and achievements bear more than a casual resemblance to those of England's "poets' poet." He broke new ground for *tz'u* poetry, rewove ancient myths and legends, turned his gaze to the small things in nature like flowers and insects; he was not restricted but rather enlarged by the conventions he inherited; and he wrote, to the very end of his life, some of the purest lyric poetry in the Chinese language.

THIRTY LYRICS BY HSIN CH'I-CHI

[GROUP A]

1 : THE CHARM OF NIEN-NU / *Nien-nu-chiao*

PRESENTED TO MAGISTRATE SHIH CHIH-TAO
upon climbing Shang-hsin Pavilion at Chien-k'ang
(1167–1170)

I have come to mourn the ancients—
To mount this lofty tower, only to reap
The grief of idle feeling a thousand measures deep!
The tiger's stance and the dragon's coil of this once great city:
    where can it be seen?
There's left only a picture of rise-and-fall to fill the eye.   5
    Homing birds by river's edge,
    Slanting sun beyond the willows,
    Tall trees soughing on the dike,
    A single sail bent westward:
Whence came the sound of a flute piercing the silence of
    autumn's bamboo grove?   10

All at once I recall the exquisite composure of Hsieh An,
His declining years spent at his Eastern Mountain retreat,
His tears falling at a harpsichord's mournful tune,
Leaving to his brothers and nephews all heroic deeds and
    fame,
His whole day consumed in a game of chess.   15
    Magic mirror of youth is hard to find,
    Clouds drift on towards dusk:
    Who needs urging to drink another cup?
The gale from the riverhead is mounting in anger,
Morning will see waves and billows tearing at houses.   20

2 : DANCE OF THE CAVALRY / *P'o-chen-tzu*

A HEROIC SONG WRITTEN FOR CH'EN T'UNG-FU
and to be sent to him
(1188)

While drunk, I trimmed my lamp and examined my sword;
In my dream, I returned to the strung-out camps and
    bugle-calls.
My soldiers feasted on roasted flesh of Eight-hundred-*li* Ox;
From fifty-string zithers came a jumble of border melodies.
    On autumn's sandy plain, I called the roll.   5

My horse flew faster than the stallion of Liu;
My bow twanged like a clap of thunder.
How I wished to discharge the kingdom's task for my prince
And to win for myself immortal fame!
    Yet how sad—my hair turns white!   10

3 : PARTRIDGE SKY / *Che-ku-t'ien*

A GUEST ARRIVED AND TALKED IMPULSIVELY
about heroic deeds and fame. I was reminded of the events
of my youth, and wrote this half in jest.
(1200)

In my youth, ten thousand brave ones rallied around my
    banners;
All splendidly-clad, fast riders fought to cross the river.
The Yen soldiers readied their silver quivers at night;
The gold-tipped arrows of Han flew at them at sunrise.

    Pondering over things of long ago,   5
      I lament my present state—
The spring wind powerless to color my white beard.
Still I would exchange my ten-thousand-word discourse on
    how to subdue the enemy
For my Eastern Neighbor's book on how to plant trees.

4 : MUSIC OF ETERNAL UNION / *Yung-yü-yüeh*

REMEMBERING THE PAST
at Pei-ku Pavilion in Ching-k'ou
(1205)

GROUP A

These enduring hills and rivers
Have left no trace of the hero,
Here in the domain of the King of Wu.
From dance terrace and song-filled pavilions,
All romance and charm have been   5
Beaten by rain, blown by the winds.
Setting sunlight on scrubby trees,
Ordinary lanes and pathways,
Where people say the royal Chi-nu once lived.
Remember those days   10
When golden lances and ironclad horses
Bolted ten thousand miles like tigers.

The debacle of the Yüan-chia era,
Vain as the hope for performing sacrifices at Lang-chü-hsü,
Only to win a retreating emperor's hasty glance.   15
Forty-three years have passed,
Yet I can still recall what I saw:
The road to Yangchow dotted by beacon-fires.
How can I bear to look back?
Beneath the temple of Buddha-fox,   20
A divine chorus of dissonant crows and temple drums.
Who shall be sent to ask:
"General Lien P'o is indeed old,
But can he really eat a peck of rice?"

[GROUP B]

1 : SONG OF THE EASTERN SLOPE / *Tung-p'o-yin*

BOUDOIR LAMENT
(date undetermined)

    Her delicate fingers pluck an ancient lament,
    Deftly tap on the embroidered board;
With a clear song, her eyes trail the geese in the west wind
    Until their formations break up, her word blown away.
    Until their formations break up, her word blown away.   5

    Deep in the night she makes her prayer to the moon
    West of the carved window.
    Only the shadow of the cassia tree
    Fills the empty stairs.
A kingfisher curtain conceals her, with no one near—   10
    Her silken garments twice as loose,
    Her silken garments twice as loose.

2 : AUSPICIOUS IMMORTAL CRANE / *Jui-ho-hsien*

ON PLUM-BLOSSOMS [*FU-MEI*]
(1191–1194)

The cold of autumn's frost pierces through the curtain
When light clouds are sheltering the moon:
    New ice still thin,
    Before the mirror brook she combs her hair;
Then thinks of dallying with scent and powder,   5
But seductive art is hard to learn.
    Pale and thin, her flesh,
    Fold upon fold
    Of colored silk, her foil.
    Relying on the east wind—   10
    One pleasant smile from her,
In a wink, ten thousand blossoms fall in shame.

Forlorn!
What place can be called her home?
Garden after a snow,
Pavilion by the water's edge,
Or an ancient assignation in Fairyland.
    Yet whom can she send
    As her courier?
GROUP B   Butterflies care only
To chase after peachtrees and willows;
The southernmost boughs laden with flowers, they do not know.
Still her heart would grieve
On some desolate evening
At the scattered sounds of the post horn.

3 : GREEN JADE CUP / *Ch'ing-yü-an*

LANTERN FESTIVAL
(before 1188)

One night's east wind and a thousand trees burst into flower;
    And breathed down still more
    Showers of fallen stars.
Splendid horses, carved carriages, fragrance filled the road.
    Music trilled from paired flutes,
    Light swirled on water-clock towers.
All night long, the fabled fish-dragons danced.

Gold-threaded jackets, moth- or willow-shaped hair-ornaments
Melted into the throng, giggling, with a trail of scents.
In the crowd I looked for her a thousand and one times;
    And all at once, as I turned my head,
    I was startled to find her
Among the lanterns where candles were growing dim.

4 : RIVER FAIRY / *Lin-chiang-hsien*
(no title given)
(date undetermined)

Her hand twirls a yellow flower, her mind blank;
Endlessly she paces the veranda, in a vacant mood.
While fragrant cassia near the rolled-up screen scatters its
    lingering scent.
  Ducks doze uneasily among withered lotus;
  Light rain in darkness fills the pond.   5

"Remembering the last time when we went hand in hand,
Now water is distant, and mountain far away.
With my silken kerchief drenched in tears, and my powdered
    face stained, we parted.
  Old pleasures in dreams anew:
  Idle and alone, I ponder them."   10

[GROUP C]

1 : THE CHARM OF NIEN-NU / *Nien-nu-chiao*

WRITTEN ON THE WALL [OF AN INN]
at Tung-liu Village
(1178)

  The wild-plum has shed all its petals;
  Once again, the season has scurried by
  Past the Ch'ing-ming Festival.
Still, the east wind deludes a traveler's dream
With a night's shiver by the mica screen.   5
  Holding a cup in hand by the winding shore,
  Or tying my horse to the weeping willow:
So many times have I taken my leave of such a place.
  The pavilion is now emptied of its guest:
Only familiar visitors, the swallows, can speak of what   10
    they knew.

    I have heard of lovely roads to the east,
    Where travelers have watched
    From beneath the curtain, maidens' mincing steps.
  Old grief, like a spring river, flows on unbroken;
  New grief stretches across a thousand clouded peaks.   15
    I imagine that some day
    When we meet again over a pot of wine,
GROUP C   Flowers in the mirror would be hard to pluck.
    Wouldn't you surprise yourself by asking,
  "How many hairs are now touched with gray?"   20

2 : GROPING FOR FISH / *Mo-yü-erh*

WRITTEN IN THE SIXTH YEAR OF CH'UN HSI
[*1179*], *upon being relieved of my duty as Assistant
Fiscal Intendant of Hupei and sent to Hunan;
at a farewell party given by my colleague Wang
Cheng-chih at Hsiao-shan* [Small Hill] *Pavilion*
(1179)

    How much more
    Of wind and rain?
  Too, too hastily, spring will leave again.
  Pitying spring, I've long dreaded flowers budding too soon.
    Still more, those fallen petals numberless!   5
    Spring, please stay!
    I've heard it said
  Fragrant grasses at world's end hide the way home.
    Uttering no word against spring,
  Except, I imagine, there must be those untiring   10
    Spiders at their web
    By painted eaves
  All day long, chafing at blown catkins.

    Alas, the Affair of Long-gate!
  Likely, the hoped-for reunion again miscarried   15
  When Delicate Beauty has earned another's spite!

True, a thousand taels of gold could buy a reconciliation;
Yet, so full and deep, to whom could this longing be told?
    Please do not dance!
    Have you not seen 20
Jade Bracelet and Flying Swallow all returned to dust?
    Bitterest sorrow is bootless grief.
    Do not lean so close against an overhanging rail,
    For where the sun has gone down
Beyond the mist and willow, is where my heart breaks! 25

3 : LOVE-SONG OF CHU YING-T'AI / *Chu-ying-t'ai-chin*

LATE SPRING
(before 1182)

    Since we halved the hairpin
    At Peach-Leaves Ferry,
Mist and willow have darkened the south bank.
    I dread to climb the upper storey:
Nine days in ten are filled with wind and rain. 5
Swirling petals, one by one, wound my heart:
    Yet others do not notice.
    And who's there to plead
With orioles to still their song?

    My hand stroked my temple, 10
Trying to divine the date of your return with petals;
The hairpin once fastened, I recounted the petals.
    Lamplight flickers on the silk curtain;
    Words choke in my mouth as I wake from dream.
"It is spring that has brought sorrow back! 15
Then where does spring go when it leaves?
    But, no, spring does not care
    To take sorrow along when it goes away."

4 : SPRING IN JADE PAVILION / *Yü-lou-ch'un*

(no title)
(date undetermined)

GROUP C

I wish to plead with the wind to let fine spring tarry;
Spring, dwelling south of the city along the flower-strewn
    road,
Has not yet followed the flowers drifting down to water's edge
But is there, where willow catkins scatter down to sodden
    ground.

Each fleck of white in the mirror tells me of what I've missed.   5
I have not wronged spring, only spring wrongs itself.
Dream vanishes, loved ones far away: that much grief
Dwells where wind and rain beat down on the pear-blossoms.

5 : FULL RIVER RED / *Man-chiang-hung*

(no title)
(date undetermined)

    Shattering the grief of separation,
    Outside the gauze window,
    The wind shook the green bamboo.
    Her lover gone,
    The sound of the flute broke off.   5
    Alone she stood by the railing.
Her eyes could not bear late April's dusk;
Her head overwhelmed by the green of a thousand hills.
    She tried to read
    One page of a letter from him,   10
    Tried to read from the beginning.

    Words of longing
    Filled the page in vain;
    Thoughts of longing—
    When would they suffice?   15
Upon her silken lapel fell tears drop after drop;
Cascades of pearls brimmed her two hands.

Fragrant grass, they say, will not hide the way home;
Hanging willows obscure the gaze only when the guest
    departs.
    Bitterest sorrow is 20
To stand and wait out the dusk as the moon goes down
    Near a winding balustrade.

6 : SPRING IN HAN PALACE / *Han-kung ch'un*

ON THE FIRST DAY OF SPRING
(1197–1198)

    Spring has returned!
Just look at spring's streamers and ribbons
Gracefully dancing on pretty maidens' heads.
    Alas, the indiscriminate wind and rain
Yet reluctant to store away the lingering cold! 5
    Seasonal swallows,
    I imagine, will this night
    Dream of returning to their orchard,
    Though unprepared to scent
The golden tangerines that go with wine 10
Among green leeks and scallions piled on the plate.

From this time on, I should laugh at the east wind
That perfumes the plum flowers and dyes the willow
    Without any let-up;
Then steal one idle moment, looking at a mirror, 15
And see the ruby color fade from my cheeks.
    Oh, interminable grief!
    Who, let me ask,
    Knows the clue to uncouple these interlocked jade-rings?
    I dread most to see
    Flowers bloom and flowers fall.
When morning comes, the frontier geese will be the first to
    come home.

[GROUP D]

1 : PURE SERENE MUSIC / *Ch'ing-p'ing-yüeh*

AFTER SPENDING A NIGHT ALONE
at the Cottage of a Certain Mr. Wang at Po-shan
(before 1188)

    Hungry rats race around my bed;
      Bats tumble and dance in lamplight.
Upon the roof, among the pines, wind spouts incessant rain
While tattered paper flaps against the window, talks by itself.

North of the border, south of the Yangtze, no stranger to me;   5
Now I am home, gray-haired, ashen-faced—
Cotton quilt, autumn night, and I lie awake:
Ten thousand miles of rivers and hills pass before my eyes.

2 : PURE SERENE MUSIC / *Ch'ing-p'ing-yüeh*

LIFE IN THE VILLAGE
(before 1188)

Thatched eaves, low and narrow;
Grass all green by the creek—
Happy with wine, the Wu dialect sounds lilting to my ear:
I wonder whose grandparents are these white-haired ones?

The oldest son hoes beans east of the creek,   5
The second boy mends the chicken coop.
I love best the youngest crafty child:
He lies by the creek breaking open lotus-pods.

3 : WEST RIVER MOON / *Hsi-chiang-yüeh*

TRAVELING THE HUANG-SHA [YELLOW-SAND]
Road at Night
(1186–1187)

Startled magpies scurrying from the branches in the moonlight,
The chittering of cicadas in midnight's cool breeze,
Talk of a bountiful year, in the fragrance of ripening grain—
The loud croaking of frogs assails my ears.

Seven or eight stars on the far horizon, 5
Two or three drops of rain closer by the hill—
A familiar wineshop by the woods beside the shrine
Appears suddenly as the road winds past the bridge.

4 : PARTRIDGE SKY / *Che-ku-t'ien*

DURING AN OUTING TO O HU [GEESE LAKE],
*I got drunk and wrote the following on the
wall of an inn.*
(1186–1187)

Spring arrives on the plain, on the petals of shepherd's purse;
Upon new furrows after the rain, a flight of crows settle.
For an old man full of feeling, what's the use of spring?
When evening comes in a wine-shop, it's easy to buy wine on
    credit.

   A leisured life, 5
   A small livelihood:
Near the cow rail to the west, there's hemp and mulberry.
Girls in blue skirts and white sleeves—I don't know where they
    are from—
To gather news about silkworms, they do visiting in the village.

5 : THE PRICKLY PEAR / *Sheng-ch'a-tzu*

VISITING YÜ-YEN [RAIN CLIFF] ALONE
(1182–1188)

GROUP D

I stroll along the stream and follow my shadow;
The sky lies at the bottom of the clear stream.
Across the sky the clouds are drifting by;
Among the drifting clouds, I find myself.

Who's there to harmonize my soaring song?   5
From hollow valleys, pure notes rise.
Not from spirits nor from immortals—
Just a song of peach-blossoms from a crescent stream.

6 : PARTRIDGE SKY / *Che-ku-t'ien*

ON THE ROAD TO HUANG-SHA
(before 1188)

A line of my verse is trimmed and shaped by the spring breeze;
Hills and streams unroll a vista like a painting.
Light-limbed sea gulls glide away on phantom boats;
Shaggy dogs turn back to greet a country woman coming home.

    Bamboo and pine,   5
      A mass of green,
Seem bent on lifting the last of snow to vie with the beauty of
    sparse plum-blossoms.
But, alas, the jumble of crows, clumsy and witless,
Time and again, kick the crystals down!

7 : BUTTERFLIES / *Fen-tieh-erh*

ON "FALLEN PLUM-BLOSSOMS,"
and Replying to a Poem Sent by
Chao Chin-ch'en
(1200)

Yesterday's spring was like
A thirteen-year-old girl learning to embroider:
    Branch after branch,
She never sketched the blossoms thin.
    Then, callously,   5
    Came down hard
    Reviling wind and rain
    Upon the garden
To carpet the ground in wrinkled red.

And now spring is like   10
A frivolous youth hard to keep at home.
    Remembering last time
    Bidding spring goodbye,
    Churning spring waves
    All into wine,   15
    A river of heady brew—
She invites the unsullied grief
To wait for her by the willow bank.

[GROUP E]

1 : UGLY SLAVE / *Ch'ou-nu-erh*

WRITTEN ON THE WALL [OF AN INN]
on the Road to Po-shan [Monastery]
(1188)

While I was young, I did not know sorrow's taste:
    I loved to climb many-storied towers.
    I loved to climb many-storied towers—
To write new rhymes and force myself to speak of grief.

THIRTY LYRICS   43

But now that I have known all of sorrow's taste,   5
    I long to speak but can't.
    I long to speak but can't—
Except to say, "What a cool autumn day!"

GROUP E   2 : UGLY SLAVE / *Ch'ou-nu-erh*

EMBELLISHING UPON SOME RHYMES
written while I was drunk, urging others to drink
(date undetermined)

Lately grief seems to grow as big as the sky.
    Who can understand and pity?
    Who can understand and pity
To make of grief as big as the sky?

I've put away endless riddles of the world, old and new,   5
    To lay them next to grief.
    To lay them next to grief
And move my home to be near Wine Spring.

3 : WEST RIVER MOON / *Hsi-chiang-yüeh*

BIDDING MY CHILDREN
to Attend to Family Affairs
(date undetermined)

Myriad affairs, like mist or cloud, as swiftly pass;
With age, the rushes and willows sear.
And now what business fits me best?
Fit to get drunk, fit to roam, fit to sleep.

Better hurry to pay your tax and levies,   5
Balance accounts and expenditure.
Your Old Sire still tends to some things—
Tends the bamboo, tends the hills, tends the lake!

4 : WEST RIVER MOON / *Hsi-chiang-yüeh*

RANDOM THOUGHTS
(date undetermined)

While drunk, I knew only to laugh and make merry;
Where's the time to grieve?
Lately, I've come to know ancient tomes,
To believe in them was all wrong.

Last night I lay drunk by the pine tree,   5
And I asked the pine, "How drunk am I?"
Half fearing the pine was moving to lift me up,
With one hand pushing the pine, I said, "Go away."

5 : SONG OF SOUTHERN VILLAGE / *Nan-hsiang-tzu*

PRESENTED TO A COURTESAN
(date undetermined)

    What a fine hostess!
Says not a word but shuffles off to bed,
Causing that man to put on airs.
    Hurry, Hurry!
Fasten your skirt, make it secure.   5

    Shed no tears of parting:
Oaths by hills and sea are hard to redeem.
Remember to take your new love today,
    My child,
Ten years later you will feel just like her.

6 : SPRING IN PRINCESS CH'IN'S GARDEN / *Ch'in-yüan-ch'un*

TRYING TO CURE MYSELF OF THE HABIT
of drinking, [I wrote this poem] to admonish the wine cup
and ask it not to come near me.
(1196)

GROUP E

    Wine-cup, you come here.
        The Old Fellow today
        Must spare his body.
For many long years I have endured this thirst;
My throat is parched like a scorched pan.   5
        And now I love to sleep;
        My snore is loud like thunder.
        You spoke of Liu Ling,
        The wisest man in history, who said,
"If I'm drunk and die, bury me where I fall."   10
    If all this were true,
I should say with a sigh, "You, my friend,
        Have been most niggardly in your affection."

Still relying on song and dance as your match-makers,
        You have conspired with them   15
        To men's doom—
Not to mention that all grudges, large and small,
        Were of addiction born.
Things are neither good nor bad;
Only excess makes calamities of them.   20
        Let this be our compact:
"Do not linger, but be quick to withdraw.
I am still strong enough to beat you down."
        Wine-cup bowed twice, and said,
        "Wave me away and I go,   25
        Call me back and I will come."

7 : [T'ANG] RIVER MESSAGE / *T'ang-ho-ch'uan*

IN IMITATION OF THE HUA-CHIEN STYLE
(date undetermined)

    Spring river,
      A thousand miles;
  A single boat among the waves:
  I dreamed of Hsi-tzu as my companion.
I woke to find dusk's sunlight deflected from the village lane.   5
      In how many homes,
    Behind low walls, hang red almond-blossoms?

From evening clouds could come a bit of rain.
      Going out to pluck flowers—
  Who is the girl on the bank?   10
    Ah, what folly!
    Over there,
    Willow catkins
Have all been swept by wind into the sky.

[GROUP F]

1 : CONGRATULATING THE BRIDEGROOM / *Ho-hsin-lang*

*I HAVE BEEN IN THE HABIT OF USING THIS
tune-title to compose poems for the gardens and pavilions of the
district. One day, while sitting alone at [the Pavilion of]
Stilled Clouds [T'ing-yün], I felt elated by the sound of
waters and the color of the hills. And I thought of similar
sentiments inspired by [other] hills and streams. Thereupon,
I wrote the following lines to approximate the mood of
longing for friends in [T'ao] Yüan-ming's [T'ing-yün] poem.*
(1199–1200)

  "Alas, alas, how much I have aged!"
     'Tis pity to see
Friends and companions fall off

        And so few of them survive today.
        My white hair has grown, in vain, thirty thousand feet 5
        When one laugh suffices for the world's myriad events!
            Ask if there's anything left
            That gladdens my heart?
        When I see green hills full of charm,
            I suspect the green hills, 10

GROUP F
        Upon seeing me, would find me the same.
            How I feel and how I look
            Should probably be alike.

Holding a flask of wine, I scratch my head before the eastern
    window
        And think of the Hermit-poet, 15
        That "Stilled Clouds" poem completed,
        Relishing a moment like this.
Those who swarm the capital, drunk with fame's lure.
Who among them can tell the subtleness of coarse wine?
        I turn my head and conjure 20
        The wind and the cloud to rise.
I bemoan, not that I haven't chanced to meet ancient worthies,
        But that the ancient worthies
    Have not chanced to see me as impertinent as this!
        None truly know me 25
        But two or three.

2 : A SLOW CHANT / *Shao-pien*

PAVILION OF AUTUMN FLOODS
[*Ch'iu-shui Kuan*]
(1199)

Inside the horn of a snail, a battle rages between
Two kingdoms: Ch'u to the left and Man to the right.
A single combat extends o'er a thousand *li* of ground.
    Try to imagine
This feeble heart encased in an inch of space! 5
Indeed, all emptiness is contained in infinitude.
    If this truth be known,

    Who can tell between Mount T'ai and a single hair?
From ancient times, heaven and earth lie in a grain of rice.
    Ah, knowing the small resemble the great,
    A turtle dove or a roc is happy with its own fate.
    What else can these two creatures know?
Remember, if Robber Chih had led a moral and just life
        Confucius would have been proven wrong;
Not to mention Infant Shang blessed with longevity and old
        P'eng-tsu ending his life in sadness.
    To expound on cold with rats unafraid of fire,
    Or to talk of heat with silkworms thriving on ice:
    Who can tell between likenesses and differences?

        Ah!
    Time decides what's noble and what's base;
    Priceless jade could only fetch a sheepskin.
    Who's able, then, to make all things equal?
        In my dream, I beheld Chuang Chou
    Tidying up the lost chapters of his writing
    And looking at me with a skittish smile.
In my empty pavilion, I woke and named it "Autumn Floods."
    A guest arrived to ask about the Great River
    Which a hundred streams had swollen with rain,
    While raging currents merged water with land's banks;
Whereupon the Lord of the River was transported with joy,
Believing that all beauty of the world belonged to him alone.
        Across the distant deep,
    He turned his gaze eastward to the ocean;
Timorously bowed to the God of the Sea and,
        in amazement, sighed,
    Saying, "If I had not met you,
    Among all Masters of Great Truth, I would not
    Have escaped being laughed at through eternity,
        after all!"
How much water can this pavilion of mine boast of?
    Only a clear stream,
    One tiny bend, that's all!

ALL translations accompanying this article follow the modern punctuated text prepared by Teng Kuang-ming, *Chia-hsüan-tz'u pien-nien ch'ien-chu* [An Annotated Edition of Chia-hsüan's *tz'u* Arranged in Chronological Order] (Shanghai: Chung Hua, 1962). Further references to this work will be abbreviated "Teng" followed by the page reference. I have also consulted the manuscript copy of both *Chia-hsüan-tz'u chiao-chu* [An Annotated Edition of Chia-hsien's *tz'u*] and *Chia hsüan-hsien-sheng nien-p'u* [Chronology of the Life of Chia-hsüan] written by Professor Cheng Ch'ien of National Taiwan University, whose many personal kindnesses I gratefully acknowledge.

Some Chinese works have been abbreviated as follows:

CST   *Ch'üan-Sung tz'u* [Complete Sung Lyrics]. T'ang Kuei-chang ed. Shanghai: Chung Hua, 1965.

HTCTC   Pi Yüan. *Hsü tzu-chih t'ung-chien* [Continuation of the Comprehensive Mirror of Perfect Administration]. 6 vols. Peking: Ku-chi ch'u-pan-she, 1957.

SPPY   *Ssu-pu pei-yao* [Essentials of the Four Libraries].

SPTK   *Ssu-pu ts'ung-k'an* [The Four Libraries].

THTP   *Tz'u-hua ts'ung-pien*. T'ang Kuei-chang ed. 12 vols. Taipei: Kwang-wen, 1967.

TSCC   *Ts'ung-shu chi-ch'eng* series. Shanghai: Commercial Press, 1940.

NOTES TO INTRODUCTION

1. *CST* collects 623 poems by Hsin Ch'i-chi. The earliest printed edition (1299) of Hsin's works contains 568 poems; an earlier manuscript edition issued during the poet's lifetime (1188 and immediately thereafter) includes 427. For a fuller account of the textual derivation of the various editions, see note 6.

2. The most extensive collection of Hsin's poems in English translation appears in Clara Candlin [Young], *The Herald Wind* (Wisdom of the East Series; London: John Murray, 1933), with nine poems (pp. 76–82), which include the poems I have translated as D_2, D_3, D_5, E_1, and E_3, and four others. Ch'u Ta-kao, *Chinese Lyrics* (Cambridge: University Press, 1937), pp. 42–48, includes seven of Hsin's poems corresponding to my D_5, E_1, E_2, E_3, and E_4, in addition to two others. In two groups of translations—"Poems from the Chinese" and "Fifty-six Poems from the Chinese"—appearing in the 1938 and 1939 *T'ien-hsia* magazine (VI, 231–254; VIII, 61–98), Teresa Li translates two of Hsin's poems: my E_2 and one other poem. *The White Pony: An Anthology of Chinese Poetry*, ed. Robert Payne (New York: John Day, 1947) includes two poems (p. 278) by Hsin corresponding to my E_1 and E_4. *A Penguin Book of Chinese Verse*, ed. A. R. Davis (Baltimore, 1962), includes only one poem by Hsin (p. 49), which is my E_1. Neither Kenneth Rexroth's *One Hundred Poems from the Chinese* (New York: New Directions, n.d.) nor Cyril Birch's *Anthology of Chinese Literature: from Early Times to the Fourteenth Century* (New York: Grove Press, 1965) includes any of Hsin's works. *A Collection of Chinese Lyrics*, by Alan Ayling and Duncan Mackintosh (London: Routledge and Kegan Paul, 1965) includes four poems by Hsin (pp. 159–67) corresponding to my A_4, C_2, C_3, and E_1. Ch'en

Shou-yi, *Chinese Literature: A Historical Introduction* (New York: Ronald Press, 1961) translates seven poems by Hsin (pp. 410–418), including my A3, C2, and E6, and three other poems. Liu Wu-chi, *An Introduction to Chinese Literature* (Bloomington: Indiana University Press, 1966) includes four poems of Hsin's translated in their entirety (pp. 121–24), which correspond to my B3, E1, and E6, and one other poem, in addition to the first stanza of my A2.

3. For a fuller treatment of the poet's life and his place in Chinese literature see my biographical and critical study, *Hsin Ch'i-chi*, in the Twayne World Authors Series (New York: Twayne Publishers, 1971).

4. Kōjirō Yoshikawa, for instance, argues for the superiority of Sung *shih* over T'ang *shih*. See his *An Introduction to Sung Poetry*, 1962 (English translation by Burton Watson; Cambridge: Harvard University Press, 1967).

5. This term was first used by James R. Hightower in *Topics of Chinese Literature* (Cambridge: Harvard University Press, 1950), p. 80. Also see Glen W. Baxter, "Metrical Origins of the *tz'u*," *Harvard Journal of Asiatic Studies*, XVII (1954), 394–402.

6. Actually, the earliest printed edition of Hsin Ch'i-chi's works was known by the title of *Chia-hsüan ch'ang-tuan-chü*, which was also the title given in the "Section on Bibliography" ("I-wen-chih") of the *History of Sung (Sung Shih, chüan* 208, p. 23a). Printed in 1299 by the Kuang-hsin Shu-yüan (Kuang-hsin Academy) of Hsin-chou (in Kiangsi), it is generally referred to as the twelve-*chüan* edition. One copy of it is still extant, in Peking; a photo reprint of this unique copy was issued by the *Ku-tien wen-hsüeh ch'u-pan-she* (Shanghai, 1957). A second printing of this edition, under the supervision of Wang Chao, in 1536, was done in Kai-feng, with punctuation of the text prepared by Li Lien (1488–1565), who also contributed a preface. It was this text, though rearranged into four-*chüan* and without Li's punctuation and preface, which was followed by Mao Chin (1598–1659) in his *Sung liu-shih ming-chia-tz'u* [Works of Sixty Famous *tz'u* Poets of Sung], reprinted in the *Ssu-pu pei-yao* [SPPY] series. Wang Pang-yün's *Sung-Yüan san-shih-i-chia tz'u* [Works of Thirty-one *tz'u* Poets of Sung and Yüan] also followed this edition.

A second major source of Hsin's works is the so-called "four-*chüan* (manuscript) edition," issued during the poet's lifetime and given the title of *Chia-hsüan-tz'u*. The four *chüan* were numbered *chia, i, ping*, and *ting*; and the *chia chüan* contained a preface which was written by Fan K'ai, one of Hsin's followers, and dated 1188. This four-*chüan* edition, content intact, was followed by Wu Na's (1372–1457) *T'ang-Sung ming-hsien pai-chia tz'u* [Works of One Hundred Worthy *tz'u* Poets of T'ang and Sung]; but a later reprint, that of Chi-ku-ko, by following an incomplete copy, reproduced only the first three *chüan*. In 1939, the *ting chüan* was miraculously rediscovered in a second-hand bookshop in Shanghai, reunited with the original, and reissued in a Han-feng-lou edition.

7. *Hua-chien chi* contains some 500 poems written by eighteen poets of the late T'ang and Five Dynasties periods, employing only 77 tune-titles. Of these, 55 were found recorded in Ts'ui Ling-ch'ing's *Chiao-fang-chi*, a T'ang collection of "Music Factory" tunes; see page three of the introduction to *Hua-chien-chi-chu*, ed. Hua Lien-p'u (Shanghai: Chung Hua, 1935). On the other hand, *The Imperial Register of Tz'u Prosody* (*Ch'ing-ting tz'u-p'u*) compiled during the K'ang-hsi reign (1662–1723), translated by Glen W. Baxter (Cambridge: Har-

vard University Press, 1956), lists 826 basic tune-titles with 2,306 variant forms (t'i), according to Baxter's tabulation (p. x). It may be significant to note that among the 77 tune-titles of the *Hua-chien chi*, only 20 are found to be included among the 101 different tune-titles used by Hsin Ch'i-chi; and only six of the 20 —"Wan-ch'i-sha," "Lang-t'ao-sha," "Lin-chiang-hsien," "P'u-sa-man," "Sheng-ch'a-tzu," and "Yü-lou-ch'un"—to have been used with some frequency (over ten poems for each of these tunes).

8. *Ch'üan-Sung tz'u*, I, 11.

9. Literally this phrase means "one who drops (*tiao*) bookbags (*shu-tai*)," where *shu-tai* is obviously a synecdoche for "erudition." Its first occurrence is in *Nan-T'ang shu* [History of the Southern T'ang (Kingdom)], by Ma Ling of the Sung dynasty, as a nickname of an eccentric named P'eng Li-yung. P'eng is said to have cultivated the habit of using quotations from the classics in his daily conversation even while he was speaking to "children and servants," *chüan* 25, *TSCC* (Shanghai: 1935), p. 167. The remark as applied to Hsin Ch'i-chi originates from the writing of Liu K'o-chuang (1187–1269), a lyricist in his own right and Hsin's follower and friend. It occurs in a "colophon" (*pa*) which Liu wrote for "Eight Lyrics on Autumn by Liu Shu-an." See "Liu Shu-an kan-ch'iu pa-shou," *Hou-ts'un ta-ch'üan-chi*, *SPTK* ed., chüan 99, p. 176.

10. For example, Chou Chi (1781–1839), *Sung ssu-chia tz'u-hsüan* [Selections from Four Sung Lyricists], 1863, reprinted in *TSCC*, considers Chou Pang-yen (1056–1121), Hsin Ch'i-chi, Wang Ch'i-sun (?1240–?1290) and Wu Wen-ying (d. 1260) as the four major lyric poets of Sung; whereas a twentieth-century view reflected in Chiang Shang-hsien, *Sung ssu-ta-chia-tz'u yen-chiu* [A Study of Four Master Lyricists of Sung] (Taipei: Ch'ung-wen, 1962) considers Su Tung-p'o, Chou Pang-yen, Hsin Ch'i-chi, and Chiang K'uei (1155–1235) as the major lyric poets of the two Sung eras.

11. Yu Yen, *Yüan-yüan tz'u-hua* (Talks on *Tz'u* from Yüan Garden], p. 2a. *THTP*, I, 349.

12. Not to mention the chronologies of the poet's life and the annotated editions of his poetry done by Liang Ch'i-ch'ao (1873–1928), Teng Kuang-ming, and Cheng Ch'ien—there have been at least six biographies of the poet published since 1946; namely, Hsü Chia-jui, *Hsin Chia-hsüan p'ing-chuan* (Chungking: Wen-t'ung, 1946); Ch'ien Tung-fu, *Hsin Ch'i-chi chuan* (Peking: Tso-chia ch'u-pan-she, 1955); Teng Kuang-ming, *Hsin Ch'i-chi chuan* (Shanghai: Jen-min ch'u-pan-she, 1956); Hsia Ch'eng-t'ao and Yu Ch'i-shui, *Hsin Ch'i-chi* (Shanghai: Chung Hua, 1962); Tu Ch'eng-hsiang, *Hsin Ch'i-chi p'ing-chuan* (Taipei: Cheng-chung, 1954); and Chiang Lin-chu, *Hsin Ch'i-chi chuan* (Taipei: Commercial Press, 1964).

13. Hu Shih, ed., *Tz'u-hsüan* (Shanghai: Commercial Press, 1927; Taipei, 1959), p. 216. Hu Shih's exact words are: "*T'a shih tz'u-chung ti-i ta-chia*," which could also be translated, without any significant change of meaning, "He is a poet of the first rank among the major *tz'u*-writers." Similar views are expressed by two other modern critics: Wang Kuo-wei (1877–1927) and Hu Yün-i. In 1910 Wang wrote in *Jen-chien tz'u-hua* (*THTP*, XII, 4252) that Hsin alone, of all the Southern Sung poets, excelled in both "self-expression" (*ch'ing*) and the "contemplation of the world" (*ching-chieh*). Hu Yün-i, in his *Sung-tz'u yen-chiu* (Shanghai: Chung Hua, 1926) wrote, "It is no exaggeration to consider Hsin Ch'i-chi as the greatest poet of Southern Sung." (p. 139)

14. Hsin's courtesy-name was Yu-an, by which he was also known; it was not until after he had moved to Ch'ien-shan, where he built his villa, that he adopted the *hao*, or style-name, of "Chia-hsüan" (which literally means "Farming Pavilion"). Descriptions of his villa can be found in the writings or the recorded conversations of several of his contemporaries—including the Neo-Confucianist philosopher Chu Hsi (1130–1200), Hung Mai (1123–1202), and Ch'en Liang.

15. According to Hsin's biography in *Sung shih* (*chüan* 401), followed by Hu Shih, Hsin's teacher was Ts'ai Sung-nien (Ts'ai Po-chien; 1107–1159); another source, originating with Yüan Hao-wen (1190–1257) *Chung-chou chi* (*SPTK* edition, *chüan* 3, p. 13b) mentions Liu Chan (Liu Yen-lao, fl. 1153) as the teacher of Hsin and Tang. This view was favored by Liang Ch'i-ch'ao and most modern biographers of Hsin.

16. The biography of Tang in *Chin shih* (History of Chin), *chüan* 125, mentions him as "the first and foremost scholar of his time" (pp. 12b–13b). Tang held many high offices including the Directorship of Education (*Kuo-tzu Chi-chiu*), membership in the Hanlin Academy, and editorship of the *Liao shih* [History of Liao]; he was also appointed Regional Commandant (*chieh-tu shih*) of T'ai-ning.

17. Hsu Meng-hua, *San-ch'ao pei-meng hui-pien* [Collectanea of Records of Treaties with the North During Three Reigns (*i.e.*, 1117–1162)], *chüan* 249, p. 5a. Reprint edition in 4 vols. (Taipei: Wen-hai, 1962), IV, 366.

18. The account in *Sung shih* agrees with what is found in *chüan* 136 of *HTCTC*, IV, 3613.

19. *Sung shih*, *chüan* 401, p. 4b. Also *HTCTC*, *chüan* 152, V, 4071.

20. This aspect of Hsin's style was briefly mentioned by Hu Yün-i, *op. cit.*, pp. 140, 142.

21. In a poem written in 1194, to the tune of "*Tsui-kao-lou*" ["The Highest Tower"]; Teng, pp. 278–79.

22. Ch'en Shu-mei, *Chia-hsüan-tz'u yung-tien feng-lei yen-chiu* [A Classified Study of the Use of Allusions in the *Tz'u* of Chia-hsien]. Unpublished M.A. thesis prepared under the direction of Professor Cheng Ch'ien (Taipei: Kuo-li Taiwan Ta-hsüeh Chung-kuo wen-hsüeh yen-chiu-so, 1967), pp. 269 ff.; pp. 251 ff.; pp. 235 ff.

23. This tune-title was specifically mentioned by Wang Cho (died 1160) in his (*Pi-chi man-chi* [Random Notes from Pi-chi], *chüan* 4, p. 3b (*THTP*, I, 65), as a T'ang title. The large number of variants of this tune are noted in Wen Ju-hsien's *Tz'u-p'ai hui-shih* [Dictionary of *Tz'u* Tune-titles] (Taipei, 1963), pp. 269–272.

24. "Problems in Translating and in Teaching Chinese Poetry," *Literature East & West*, vol. VII, Nos. 2 and 3 (1963), 29–58.

25. Ch'en Shu-mei, *op. cit.*, lists 34 allusions to, or quotations from *The Analects*; 17 from the *Book of Mencius*; and 89 from *Chuang-tzu* (pp. 161–65; 165–67; 221–30).

26. *Milton's Prose*, ed. Malcolm W. Wallace (London: Oxford University 1925; 1942), p. 154.

27. Ch'en Shu-mei, *op. cit.*, p. 153, where she lists 44 allusions to, or quotations from the *Shih ching*.

NOTES TO POEMS

GROUP A / POEM I

TUNE-TITLE: Teng, p. 11. This tune-title is said to have been derived from a song singing the praise of a famous courtesan by the name of Nien-nu, the rage of the T'ang capital during the T'ien-pao period (742–756). See Wang Cho's (d. 1160) *Pi-chi Man-chi* [Random Talks from Pi-chi], *chüan* 5, p. 1a (*THTP*, I, 73).

TITLE: Shih Cheng-chih, whose courtesy-name was Chih-tao, passed the *chin-shih* examination in 1151 and was made the Magistrate of Chien-k'ang (modern Nanking in Kiangsu) in 1167. Convinced of the strategic importance of Chien-k'ang, Shih once attempted to persuade Emperor Kao-tsung to make it his capital instead of Ling-an.

line 4 "tiger's ... coil": The text reads *hu-chü lung-pang* (literally, to stand there like a tiger and to coil like a dragon) referring to the city of Nanking and its surrounding hills, the Chung Mountains. The quotation is attributed to Chu-ke Liang, the strategist of the Shu kingdom, who praised the city, then the capital of Wu (222–264), in these words.

line 10 "sound ... grove": Alluding to a line from a lyric by Huang T'ing-chien (1045–1105), to the tune of "The Charm of Nien-nu" written on the subject "Awaiting the moon's arrival on the seventeenth day of the eighth month, in the company of several nephews and a famous flutist." (*CST*, p. 385)

line 11 "Hsieh An": The text reads *An-shih*, the courtesy-name of Hsieh An (320–385), a man known for his elegant manners and sagacity. The poem refers to the following story about his composure. In 383 the huge army of Fu Chien, a Tibetan general who had become the ruler of the Earlier Ch'in Kingdom, was defeated by Hsieh An's nephew Hsieh Hsüan (343–388) and Hsieh Shih (327–388), his younger brother; and the news was brought to him while he was playing chess. He did not allow the message to interrupt his game; and only when the game was over he remarked, "Our children (hsiao-erh-pei) have broken up the rebels." *Chin-shu chiao-chu* [History of Chin Dynasty, Collated and Annotated].

A 2

Teng, p. 204. Conjecturally dated 1188, a deduction supported by a letter from Ch'en to the poet, dated "the year of *wu-shen* [i.e., 1188]," in which Ch'en asked Hsin for some poems. See Cheng Ch'ien, *Chia-hsien-tz'u chiao-chu*, p. 198.

Ch'en Liang (?1143–1192), whose courtesy-name was T'ung-fu, was a very close friend of the poet and one whose political view Hsin shared. In the 1160's Ch'en memorialized the throne with "five discourses" for "revitalizing the kingdom" (*Chung-hsing-wu-lün*), but his recommendations were rejected. He passed the *chin-shih* examination during Emperor Kuang-tsung's reign (1190–1194), and left two volumes of collected works: *Lung-ch'uan Tz'u* and *Lung-ch'uan Wen-chi*.

line 3 "Eight-hundred-*li* Ox": An allusion to a story found under the topic of "Extravagances" (*chüan* 30) in a famous fifth-century collection of anecdotes, Liu I-ch'ing's (403–444) *Shih-shuo hsin-yü*. The story concerns a wager between a noted archer, who also owned a rare ox named "Eight-hundred-*li* Beast (*po*)," and his friend who, professing to be less skilled in archery, wagered a huge sum of money against the ox if he should miss the target in a match. The friend was first to shoot, and after he hit the mark, he nonchalantly said, "Fetch me the heart of the animal."

line 4 "fifty-string zithers": Alluding to the "Ornamented Zither" poem by the T'ang poet Li Shang-yin (813–858). See James J. Y. Liu, *The Poetry of Li Shang-yin* (Chicago: University of Chicago Press, 1969), pp. 51–57.

line 6 "horse of . . . Liu": The text reads *Ti-lu*, the name of a stallion owned by Liu Pei, the founder of the Shu kingdom during the Three Kingdoms period.

A 3

TUNE-TITLE: Teng, pp. 392–93.

line 3 "silver quivers": The text reads "*yin* (silver) *hu-lu*." The latter, besides being a rhyming-compound, is an archaic term for "arrow," following *Hsin T'ang Shu* (New History of T'ang, *chüan* 13, p. 2b), "Record on Ceremonies" (*I-wei-Chih*).

line 4 "gold-tipped arrows": The text reads "*chin* (gold) *p'u-ku*," actually the proper name of an arrow used by Duke Chuang of Lu to shoot and capture a disloyal minister of the Sung kingdom named Nan-kung Chang-wan, as recorded in the *Tso Chuan* (Commentary According to Tso on the Spring and Autumn Annals). See James Legge's *The Chinese Classics*, 5 vols. (Hongkong, 1872; 1960), vol. V, pp. 87, 88, where this name is romanized as "Kin Puh-koo" and tentatively translated as "Steel Servant-lady." Since lines 3-4 require strict parallelism, most probably the use of this archaism, another rhyming compound, was more than to suggest a historical parallel: it was also to achieve auditory effect, as well as a visual one in the two contrastive words (gold and silver) immediately preceding these two terms.

line 5 "things of long ago": According to the poet's biography in Sung History (*Sung shih*), upon the death of the Chin ruler Hai-ling-wang (reigned 1149–1161), there had been numerous anti-Jurchëd uprisings in Shantung, one of which was led by Ken Ching. Hsin joined Ken's forces as a secretary and was sent to have an audience with Emperor Kao-tsung, held in Chien-k'ang in 1162. Upon his return to the rebel base, he discovered that Ken had been betrayed and murdered by one of his followers who subsequently surrendered to the Chin army. Suspecting the whereabouts of this culprit, Chang An-kuo, the poet led a posse to raid the enemy camp, dragged Chang away from a feast, escaped, and later had Chang executed at a marketplace. (*chüan* 401, 1b–2a)

line 8 "still": For the first word of this line, *ch'üeh*, I follow Teng and the twelve-*chüan* edition, a variant of which, found in the four-*chüan* edition and followed by *CST* is *tu*, meaning "*all*." An intensifier-particle, "*ch'üeh*" in the sense of "*huan*" or "*ren*," meaning "still" or "yet," occurs quite often in the works of Tu Fu, in the lyrics of Hsin's contemporaries, and in Hsin's other poems. This meaning appears justifiable by the title.

line 9 "Eastern Neighbor": Borrowed from the story of Wang Chi found in *Ch'ien Han-shu* [History of Former Han], *chüan* 72, p. 7b. The wife of the young scholar Wang served her husband dates that had fallen from the tree of their neighbor to the east. Wang was ashamed when he discovered his wife's behavior and wanted to divorce her. His neighbor, however, diplomatically suggested that the tree be cut down. The villagers also pleaded with Wang to take back his wife. Wang ultimately agreed. The story is not relevant to the poem and is used solely for embellishment in a manner which modern Chinese critics found objectionable.

A4

TUNE-TITLE: Teng, p. 527.
TITLE: Modern Chen-chiang in Kiangsu. The Pei-ku ("Northern Firmness") Pavilion, situated north of Ching-k'ou (modern Chen-chiang in Kiangsu), overlooks the Yangtze from the top of a high mountain. It was built by Ts'ai Mo in the Chin dynasty and later repaired by Hsieh An. Cf. Ku Tzu-yu's *Tu-shih fang-yü chi-yao*, *chüan* 25 (Shanghai: Chung Hua, 1955), 6 vols., p. 1178.
line 3 "King of Wu": The text reads "Sun Chung-mo," the courtesy-name of Sun Ch'üan, founder of the Wu kingdom (reigned 222-252).
line 9 "royal Chi-nu": The nickname of Liu Te-yü (Liu Yü) who later became the founder of the (Southern) Sung kingdom and was known as Wu-ti (reigned 420-422). Before his usurpation, which ended the Chin dynasty, he lived in Ching-k'ou as a subject.
line 13 "debacle . . . era": Yüan-chia is the reign title of the third ruler of the (Southern) Sung kingdom, who was known as Wen-ti (reigned 424-454) and who waged frequent disastrous military campaigns against the Northern (Toba) Wei dynasty (386-451). The text for this line reads *Yüan-chia ts'ao-ts'ao* (literally, Yüan-chia hastily), meaning "The plans of the Yüan-chia era so hastily drawn up."
line 14 "vain . . . Lang-chü-hsü": The text of this line reads: *feng Lang-chü-hsü* (literally, to be enfeoffed at Mount Lang-chü-hsü). Mount Lang-chü-hsü was a mountain given to the famous general Huo Ch'ü-ping (B.C. 145-117) by Han Wu-ti as a reward for his victory over the Huns (*Shih chi chüan* 111; p. 2396). But the line actually alludes to a later story of the Sung kingdom: Wang Hsien-mo (died 468) was so eager to engage the enemy, the Northern Wei, that the Emperor is said to have remarked, "To listen to Hsien-mo talk makes one wish to perform sacrifices at Mount Lang-chü-hsü," *Sung shu* (History of the Sung [Kingdom]), 76/5a. In ancient China, emperors or their deputies periodically offered sacrifices to sacred or famous mountains as an act of homage to Heaven.
line 16 "Forty-three years": This bit of internal evidence for dating this poem, in the poet's reference to the events of 1162, has been corroborated by an entry entitled "Chia-hsüan Lun Tz'u" (Chia Hsüan's Discourse on *Tz'u*) found in Yüeh K'o's (1173-?1240) *T'ing shih* (*chüan* 3, pp. 16a-19a) where this poem is referred to as Hsin's "new composition."

Yüeh wrote that Hsin was fond of having courtesans sing his lyrics. He often unhesitatingly expressed his satisfaction with the lines he thought most successful after the courtesan sang one of his works; and he was in the habit of urging his guests to offer criticism. On this occasion, a party, Hsin finished commenting on his own work, mentioning his pleasure at the opening and closing lines of this poem and repeatedly urged Yüeh to comment. After several polite attempts to avoid answering, Yüeh ventured the remark: "Your poem indeed expresses the most heroic of sentiments, but the key lines at the beginning and at the end of the poem seem too much alike, and your new composition seems to me to contain too many allusions." (p. 18a) Upon hearing this remark, the poet was greatly pleased and said, "You have really discovered my worst addiction [*ku*, which also has the meaning of "a chronic disease"]!" Yüeh stated that this party took place in the year of "I-ch'ou," or 1200, while he was journeying to the capital to take his palace examination.

line 20 "Buddha-fox": "Buddha-fox," or Fo-li, was the pet name of the third emperor of Northern Wei, known as T'ai-wu-ti (reigned 424–451), whose cruelty and boldness made him much feared by the (Southern) Sung kingdom against whom he waged many successful military campaigns.

lines 22–24 "Who . . . rice?": Lien P'o was a famous general during the Warring States period, whom the king of Chao had wanted to employ against Ch'in. The king sent an emissary to find out if the general was too old to serve; suspecting this design, Lien demonstrated his fitness before his guest by consuming in one meal a peck of rice and ten catties of meat. However, the emissary, bribed by Lien's enemy, reported to the king saying, "The general could still eat rice, but during the short time of our conversation he had to go out to urinate three times." The king of Chao gave up his plan of employing Lien P'o. (*Shih chi*, *chüan* 81; pp. 2448–2449 in the 1959 Chung Hua reprint edition.)

B1

TUNE TITLE: Teng, p. 504.

TITLE: This title was not found in either the twelve-*chüan* or the four-*chüan* edition, but was suggested by Wang Chao in the second printing of the twelve-*chüan* text in 1536.

line 3 "geese": In Chinese poetry, the flight of the geese is associated with the grief and longing of separation because of the regularity, and hence the faithfulness, of their migratory habit. Their formation, which takes the shape of the character for "man" (*jen*) also comes to symbolize letters or messages.

line 8 "cassia tree": *i.e.*, the cassia tree which according to legend grows inside the moon.

B2

TUNE TITLE: Teng, pp. 280–81.

line 1 "autumn's frost": The text reads *yen-shuang* (literally "wild-geese frost"), with *yen* suggestive of the season of autumn when wild geese fly south.

line 17 "Fairyland": The text reads "*yao-ch'ih*," or Jasper Pond, which was mentioned in an ancient legend as the meeting place between King Mu of Chou (of tenth century B.C.) and the Queen Mother of the West, who conferred immortality upon the emperor. (*Mu-t'ien-tzu chuan*, SSPY edition, *chüan* 3, pp. 1a–1b)

B3

TUNE TITLE: Teng, pp. 188–89.

TITLE: "Yüan-hsi," or "*yüan-hsiao*," celebrated on the fifteenth day of the first month of the lunar year. In Sung times the lantern festival lasted three days, and was later extended to five.

line 3 "Showers . . . stars": A day-by-day account of the festivities of the three-day period in the capital of the Northern Sung is given in *chüan* 6 of Meng

Yüan-lao's (*fl.* 1126) *Tung-Ching Meng-hua-lu* [Recollections of the Splendor of the Eastern Capital] published in 1147. Under the entry of the sixteenth day, it is recorded that from bamboo poles and "far and near, high and low, they appeared like flying stars." (Pp. 180–83 in the annotated edition by Teng Chi-ch'eng [Shanghai: Commercial Press, 1959].)

line 5 "paired flutes": The text reads *feng-hsiao* or "phoenix-flute," made of small bamboo pipes which were laid in uneven rows and therefore said to resemble the wings of the phoenix.

line 7 "fish dragons": Referring to lantern-dances in general. The term "yü-lung," or "fish dragon," is borrowed from Yen Shih-ku's annotations of *Ch'ien-Han shu* [History of Former Han], *chüan* 96b, p. 38a, where it is identified as a dance imported from Central China in which Han emperors took great delight. "Yü-lung" was said to be an exotic animal from "She-li," which first played in the courtyard, then jumped into water to become a fish with two pairs of eyes and finally emerged as a yellow dragon eighty feet long. The celebration of this dance on the fifteenth day of the first month was discontinued in the Later Han dynasty.

line 8 "moth . . . ornaments": Hair-ornaments in the shapes of the moth, bee, or willow were common objects for sale at the booths during the Festival, as mentioned in Meng, *op. cit.*, and in *Ta-Sung Hsüan-ho Yi-shih* (Recollections of Events of the Hsüan-ho Period of Great Sung), an anonymous work of the Sung-Yüan period, under the entry for the 6th year of Hüsan-ho [1124], for the fourteenth day of the first month.

B4

TUNE TITLE: Teng, pp. 469–70.

C1

TUNE TITLE: Teng, pp. 46–47.

line 1 "wild-plum": The text in both the twelve-*chüan* and the four-*chüan* editions reads "t'ang," meaning a wild-plum or crab-apple tree. Wang Chao, in the 1536 reprint edition of the former, changed the character to one that also reads "T'ang" but means "creek," an emendation followed by Mao Chin and some other editors. If this interpretation is accepted, line one of this poem ("yeh-t'ang-hua-lo") can also be translated to read: "Petals have fallen on deserted creeks."

line 3 "Ch'ing-ming": Clear-and-Bright Festival (Ch'ing-ming chieh) usually occurs in the first week of April in China, when families often go to the countryside to visit ancestral graves.

C2

TUNE TITLE: Teng, p. 55.

TITLE "Wang cheng-chih": Wang Cheng-chi (died 1192), whose courtesy-name was Cheng-chih, was an official known for his high integrity. Later made Lord of the Imperial Treasury (*t'ai-fu-ch'ing*), he served the empire while both his father, Wang Hsün, and his two brothers were prominent officials. Cf. Lou Yüeh's (1137–1213) *Kung-k'uei chi*, SPTK edition, *chüan* 99, pp. 15b–21a; *chüan* 100, pp. 1a–7b.

"Hsiao-shan Pavilion": Located near the official residence in O-chou, Hupei. See Wang Hsiang-chih's *Yü-ti chi-sheng* [Record of Famous Places in Empire], *chüan* 66, p. 5b.

line 14: The allusion is to Ssu-ma Hsiang-ju (179–117 B.C.), a gifted writer of *fu*, to whom *Ch'ang-men Fu* ("On the Long-gate Palace") was attributed. The central theme of the work is the grief of a rejected woman. According to legend, this composition was commissioned at the price of "a hundred catties of gold" by Empress Ch'en when she was out of favor with Emperor Wu-ti; and she regained her position as a result of his reading it.

line 16 "Delicate Beauty": The text reads "o-mei," or "moth-brow," a standard epithet for either a woman's beauty or the beauty of a man's moral character as used in *Li Sao* (line 45).

line 17 "reconciliation": For "reconciliation," the text reads "Hsiang-ju's *fu*."

line 21 "Jade . . . Swallow": Referring to Yang Kuei-fei, whose nickname was Yü Huan (Jade Bracelet), and to Chao Fei-yen (Flying Swallow)—respectively imperial concubines of T'ang Ming-huang and Han Ch'eng-ti.

C3

TUNE TITLE: Teng, p. 83. The last word *chin* in a song-title usually means "with an extra syllable added to the original tune." But in this case, both "*Chu-ying-t'ai*" and "*Chu-ying-t'ai-chin*" have the same number of words (77). The pattern originated with Hsin, and it must have become immediately popular since some of his younger contemporaries, like Liu Kuo and Yüeh K'o, and many later lyricists, including Chang Yen and Wu Wen-ying, wrote to this tune. The use of this tune-pattern was obviously suggested by the theme of the poem; the name in the tune-title came from a still popular Chinese love story dating back to the Eastern Chin dynasty. According to this story, Liang Shan-po as a boy fell in love with a schoolmate named Chu Ying-t'ai, who for three years disguised herself as a boy. Later when Liang discovered her true identity and asked for her hand in marriage, he learned that she had already been betrothed. Still later, after becoming a magistrate, Liang fell ill and left specific instructions as to where he must be buried. On her wedding day, Chu's boat passed by that spot and a storm broke out. She left the boat to pay a visit to Liang's grave, and as she reached the graveside the ground broke asunder; she leaped in and killed herself. *Chüan* 36 of *Ningpo Gazette*; *Ning-po-fu chih*, 4 vols., ed. Ts'ao Ping-jen (Taipei, 1957), p. 2618.

line 1 "halved the hairpin": Referring to the pledge of love exchanged between Yang Kuei-fei and T'ang Ming-huang, with each of them keeping half of the pair of ornamented hairpins. Cf. Po Chü-i's *Ch'ang-heng-ko* (Song of Everlasting Sorrow).

line 2: "Peach-Leaves" (T'ao-yeh) was said to have been the name of the concubine of the poet Wang Hsien-chih (344–397), who said goodbye to her with a song at a ferry also named T'ao-yeh. The song is included in *Ku-shih hsüan* (Selections of Ancient Poetry), *chüan* 5, p. 6a.

line 11 "petals": *i.e.*, petals of flowers secured on hairpins worn by women as ornaments. The act of counting the numbers of petals to see if they agree with a number chosen at random probably refers to a superstition or game which is often resorted to by people trying to guess at an answer to a difficult personal question.

C4

TUNE TITLE: Teng, p. 482.

line 5 "each fleck of white": The text reads *"hsing-hsing,"* literally "star (upon) star," here meaning white hair—as numerous as stars.

C5

TUNE TITLE: Teng, p. 455.

C6

TUNE TITLE: Teng, p. 463.

line 2 "streamers and ribbons": The text reads *ch'un-fan* (literally, spring pennants). According to a contemporaneous account, it was the custom on the first day of spring for the gentlefolks of the Eastern Capital, K'ai-feng, to cut colorful paper into pennants and streamers and display them as hair-ornaments or hang them from trees. See Meng Yüan-lao (*fl.* 1126), *Tung-ching meng-hua lu* [Recollections of the Splendor of the Eastern Capital, i.e. K'ai-feng], 1147 (Shanghai, 1956), p. 172.

D1

TUNE TITLE: Teng, p. 135.

D2

Teng, p. 190.

D3

Teng, p. 250.

D4

Teng, p. 152.

D5

Teng, pp. 142–43.

TITLE: The word "alone" (*tu*) does not appear in the four-*chüan* edition.

"Rain Cliff," which appears in the titles of numerous poems written by the poet during his first period of residence at Shang-jao, where he built his villa, is a name that does not turn up in any of the gazettes and geographical accounts of Sung times, although Shang-jao and its adjacent areas were known for their scenic beauty. It has only been tentatively identified as Rain Stone Mountain (*Yü-shih Shan*), which is mentioned in *Yü-ti chi-sheng*, *chüan* 21, p. 5a and located about 15 miles southeast of Yung-feng *hsien*.

line 5 "harmonize": The word *"ho,"* meaning "to echo" or, in the technical usage of poetry, "to exchange a poem with someone else, usually using the same rhymes."

line 8: This line *i-ch'ü t'ao-hua-shui* can be translated more literally as either "one bend of peach-blossoms water" or as "one song of peach-blossoms water." My translation assumes that there might have been a pun concealed in the word *ch'ü*, which has two common meanings: (1) a dramatic song and (2) a winding body of water. The last three words make up an ambiguous phrase which is said by one scholar to refer to the reflection in the water of peachtrees growing on the banks (Hu Shih, *Tz'u-hsüan* [Shanghai, 1927; Taipei, 1959], p. 233). Another translator prefers to think of the peach-blossoms as floating on the water; see Ch'u Ta-kao, *Chinese Lyrics* (Cambridge, England: Cambridge University Press, 1937), p. 45. The line, incidentally, may be considered as a good illustration of synesthesia in Chinese poetry, since the poet employs in one line all three senses: the auditory, the visual, and the olfactory.

D 6

Teng, p. 250.

D 7

Teng, p. 403.
TITLE: "Chao Chin-ch'en": Chao Pu-yü, whose courtesy-name was Chin-ch'en, earned his *chin-shih* degree in 1154; and he retired to Shang-jao, where he was known to have built at least two pavilions and to have been fond of writing poetry. Cf. "Biography of Resident Worthies" (*Yü-hsien-chuan*) in the Gazette of Shang-jao *hsien* (*Shang-jao-hsien-Chih*), quoted in Teng, p. 371. The poet exchanged many poems with him during his second period of residence at Shang-jao.

E 1

Teng, p. 137.

E 2

Teng, p. 497.
TITLE: The title for this poem is tentatively supplied from the one given for an immediately preceding poem written to the same tune, and also on account of the subject-matter, which is identical in both poems.
line 8 "Wine Spring": Chiu-ch'üan," or Wine Spring, is a fabled city known since Han times for the underground spring of the district called "Golden Spring" (*chin-ch'üan*) which supposedly tastes like wine. Cf. Tu Fu's "*Yin-chung pa-hsien-ko*" ("Eight Immortals of the Wine Cup," English translation by William Hung in his *Tu Fu: China's Greatest Poet* (Cambridge: Harvard University Press, 1952), pp. 51–52, which also uses this allusion.

E 3

Teng, pp. 432–33.

E 4

Teng, pp. 486–87.

E 5

Teng, p. 471.

E 6

Teng, p. 312.
line 8 "Liu Ling": Liu Ling (?221–300) was one of the Seven Worthies of the

Bamboo Grove, said to have been inordinately fond of drinking. Anecdotes about his habits and idiosyncrasies are generously mentioned in Liu I-ch'ing's (403-444) *Shih-shuo hsin-yü* [New Account of the Tales of the World], one of the poet's favorite books. The quotation in line 10 was taken from Liu Hsiao-piao's (462-521) annotations to one of the entries on Liu Ling in this book in *chüan* 2. According to this account, Liu used to ride on a deer-cart which he would load with wine. A servant with a shovel always accompanied him with instructions that he should be buried wherever he happened to die. (Liu I-ch'ing, *Shih-shuo hsin-yü chu*, Hong Kong reprint edition: Tai-p'ing, 1966, p. 61) Also cf. *chüan* 5 (p. 179).

E7

Teng, p. 507.

This tune-title, generally known as "*Ho-ch'uan*," is among the oldest of *tz'u* tunes and the most popular among both the *Hua-chien* poets (see Introduction) and Sung lyricists. It is also the most irregular with respect to rhyme scheme, line length and the number of words in each line. Among the eighteen poets included in the *Hua-chien Chi*, seven poets—Chang Pi, Wen T'ing-yün, Sun Kuang-hsien, Yen Hsüan, Wei Chuang, Ku Hsiung and Li Hsün—wrote to this tune, using from 51 to 55 words in different variations (*t'i*). Hsin in this poem used 53 words; whereas other Sung lyricists—including Liu Yung, Chang Hsien, and Ch'in Kuan—added extra words to as many as 61. Cf. Wen Ju-hsien, *Tz'u-p'ai hui shih* (Taipei, 1963), pp. 269-72. One of Chang Pi's two poems written to this tune in the *Hua-chien Chi* begins with the following line: "How vast is the water under the cloud" ("*Miao-man yün-shui*," *chüan* 4, p. 9a); the other begins with the two words "*hung-hsing*," or "red almond-blossoms" (p. 9b). It is possible that Hsin attempted to parody these two poems in particular as well as the *Hua-chien* style in general.

TITLE: Instead of *t'i* or style, the four-*chüan* edition reads *chi*, which means "collection" or "anthology."

line 4 "Hsi-tzu": Hsi-tzu, or Hsi Shih, was a famous beauty of the fifth century B.C.

F1

Teng, pp. 338-39.

TITLE "Ting-yün" poem: In Hsin's villa, the poet named one of the pavilions "T'ing-yün," after the title of one of T'ao Ch'ien's (T'ao Yüan-ming) poems, which must have been among Hsin's favorite reading since he had elsewhere (Teng, pp. 331-32) paraphrased and expanded this four-word poem into a *tz'u*. In this poem of T'ao's there are the following lines: "There is wine, there is wine,/ Let us drink leisurely before the eastern window" (*Ching-chieh hsien-sheng chi*, *chüan* 1, pp. 1a-2a); hence the allusion in line 14.

line 1: Taken verbatim from *The Analects* of Confucius (V.v).

line 5: "My white hair, thirty thousand feet long/ My grief is as long as that" are the opening lines of Li Po's "*Ch'iu-p'u ko*" [Song from the Autumn Banks], No. 15 (*Li T'ai-po shih-chi*, SPPY edition, *chüan* 8, p. 3a). The line reads *pai-fa san-ch'ien-chang* (literally "white hair three thousand *chang*"), *chang* being a measure word for ten feet. Hsin borrows this hyperbole and breaks up the line by adding two words in the middle; *k'ung ch'ui* (literally "in vain").

line 15 "Hermit poet": The text reads "*Yüan-ming*," the courtesy-name of T'ao Ch'ien.

line 18 "the capital": The text reads "*chiang-tso*," meaning "left of the river"; i.e., on the eastern bank of the Yangtze where the capital of the Chin dynasty —Chien-k'ang, or Nanking,—was located. The phrase first occurs in the Biography of Wen Ch'iao (288–329) in *Chin-shu* [History of the Chin Dynasty], *chüan* 67, p. 2a. As a spirited young man, before his rise to prominence, Wen was said to have complimented the then prime minister Wang Tao, who served Emperor Yüan (reigned 317–323), by saying ,"Since there is Kuan I-wu [*i.e.* Kuan Chung, a famous minister of Ch'i during the Warring States period] on the left of the river, what is there for me to worry about?" Under Emperor Ch'eng (326–343), Wen Ch'iao distinguished himself as a general and was later made Duke of An-chün. Wen was responsible for crushing several rebellions and served as a colleague of T'ao K'an (257–332), the great-grandfather of the poet T'ao Ch'ien.

line 19 "subtleness of coarse wine": For "coarse wine" the text reads: *cho-lao* (*cho* meaning "the turbid or muddy of wine" and *lao* meaning "the dregs of wine").

line 21 "wind and cloud": Alluding to the famous lines of Han Kao-tsu, the first emperor of Han: "The great wind rises and the clouds are scattered . . ./ Where can I find brave warriors to guard the far corners of the empire?" (Ting, p. 1). There are only two short poems attributed to Han Kao-tsu, the other being the "Song of the Great Swan" ("Hung-ku ko").

lines 22–24 "I . . . this": With the exception of the word "impertinent" (*k'uang*), these lines, so much admired by Hsin's contemporaries, appear to contain an allusion to a statement attributed to Chang Yung (444–497), known for his literary brilliance while still a young man. In the official biography of Chang, it is said, "he often sighed and said, 'I do not regret, or bemoan (*heng*) that I have not met the ancient worthies; what I really regret, or bemoan, is that the ancient worthies have not met me'." (*Nan shih*, 32/13a).

line 26: Taken *verbatim* from *The Analects* (V.xxv).

F 2

Teng, p. 342.

TITLE: "*Ch'iu-shui*," the name the poet chose for his pavilion, is the title of the 17th chapter of the Works of the Taoist philosopher Chuang-tzu, or Chuang Chou (line 22). The naming of this pavilion, constitutes the subject matter of this lyric. In his 17th chapter, Chuang-tzu expounds the idea that conceit comes from ignorance, with a parable which tells about a river swollen by the autumn floods and becoming arrogant until it meets the ocean when it becomes convinced of its smallness.

Besides the many allusions and a parable which begins the poem, the chief device used in this lyric is a kind of dream-allegory, which makes this poem quite similar to Coleridge's *Kubla Khan*, although Hsin's poem is cast in a metaphysical vein. At the same time, its philosophical overtones may remind Western readers of T. S. Eliot's "The Dry Salvages" in his *Four Quartets*, which also deals with the themes of space and time. Cf. the following lines from Eliot: "The river is within us, the sea is all about us . . ./ and under the oppression of the silent fog/ The tolling bell/ Measures time not our time, rung by the un-

hurried/ Ground swell, a time/ Older than the time of chronometers. . . ."
(*The Complete Poems and Plays* [New York: Harcourt, Brace, 1930], pp. 130–31)

Since Chuan-tzu's writings are available in many English translations, I shall identify the allusions to this chapter and other chapters by quoting from the translation of James Legge, *The Texts of Taoism* (New York: Julian Press, 1959) except that the romanization of Chinese names will follow the Wade-Giles system.

line 2: This parable is taken from the 25th ("*Tse-yang*") chapter of *Chuang-tzu*, occurring in the middle of a dialogue. "'There is the creature called a snail; does your majesty know it?' 'I do.' 'On the left horn of the snail, there is a kingdom which is called Provocation [*i.e.* Ch'u], and on the right horn another which is called Stupidity [*i.e.* Man]. These two kingdoms are continually striving about their territories and fighting. The corpses that lie on the ground amount to several myriads. The army of the one may be put to flight, but in fifteen days it will return'." (Legge, p. 559)

line 8 "Mount T'ai": Mount T'ai, or T'ai-shan, was one of the sacred mountains in ancient China. This comparison comes from the 2nd chapter of *Chuang-tzu* entitled "Ch'i-wu-lun" (A Discourse on the Equalizing of Things). The allusion is to the following passage, "Under heaven there is nothing greater than the tip of an autumn down, and the T'ai mountain is small." (Legge, p. 236)

line 9: This comparison comes from the following passage in the "*Ch'iu-shui*" chapter: ". . . if we call those great which are greater than others, there is nothing that is not great, and in the same way there is nothing that is not small. We shall (thus) know that heaven and earth is but (as) a grain of the smallest rice. . . ." (Legge, p. 427)

line 11: The parable about how a huge bird called a "roc" (*p'eng*) appeared to a turtle dove and a cicada comes from the first chapter of *Chuang-tzu* entitled "*Hsiao-yao-yu*" (Free and Easy Wandering). The allusion is made to the following passages: "In the Northern Ocean there is a big fish . . . I do not know how many *li* in size. It changes into a bird with the name of P'eng, the back of which is (also) I do not know how many *li* in extent. . . . [It ascended to] the height of 90,000 *li* and there was such a mass of wind beneath it. As it seemed to bear the blue sky on its back . . . a cicada and a little dove laughed at it, saying, 'We make an effort and fly towards an elm or sapanwood tree; and sometimes before we reach it, we can do no more but drop to the ground. Of what use is it for this (creature) to rise 90,000 *li* . . . ?' He who goes to the grassy suburbs . . . will have his belly as full as when he set out; he who goes to a distance of 100 *li* will have to pound his grain where he stops for the night; he who goes a thousand *li*, will have to carry with him provisions for three months. What should these two creatures know about the matter?" (Legge, pp. 212–14)

line 12: This line is taken *verbatim* from *Chuang-tzu*. See note to line 11.

line 14: This allusion is made to an apocryphal story about Confucius' meeting with a notorious robber named Chih; among other places, it also appears in the 29th chapter of *Chuang-tzu* entitled "Tao Chih" (Robber Chih). See Legge, pp. 606–626.

line 16: This paradox is found in the 2nd chapter of *Chuang-tzu*; Legge's translation reads "There is no one longer-lived than a child which dies prematurely, and P'eng-tsu did not live out his time." (p. 236) "Infant Shang" is my literal translation of "Shang-tzu," which can be paraphrased in more than one way. Burton Watson's translation, as found in *Chuang Tzu: Basic Writings* (New York: Columbia University Press, 1964), reads as follows: "No one has lived longer than a dead child, and P'eng-tsu died young." (p. 38) *Shang* is a word used in ancient China to refer to the death of a person under nineteen years old. Since customs and concepts differ as to what constitutes "an untimely death," I have translated these two words literally. P'eng-tsu, the Chinese Methuselah, is said to have lived to 700–800 years.

line 17: This reference to a bit of Chinese "unnatural natural history" is contained in a book entitled *Wu-lü* cited by *T'ai-p'ing-yü-lan*, a Sung encyclopedia compiled under Imperial auspices by Li Fan (925–996). The passage may be translated as follows: "In Pi-ching *hsien* of Jih-nan, there grow fire-rats whose hair can be woven into cloth which does not burn in fire. Hence, the cloth is called "huo-wan-pu," or Cloth-washed-by-fire." (*chüan* 820, p. 8a; p. 3651 in the 1960 Chung-hua reprint edition)

line 18: This information comes from a passage in *chüan* 10 of *Shih-yi-chi* [Record of Lost or Forgotten Events], as quoted in Teng, p. 343, which I have translated as follows: "In Yüan-ch'iao-shan, or Mount Yüan-ch'iao, there is a kind of ice-silkworm. Its cocoon forms only after it has been covered up with frost and snow. Over one foot long, it has brilliant colors. After it has been woven into silk, the silk does not dissolve in water; thrown into fire, it will not burn even after one night."

line 22: The first two words of this line in the original text read "Lien-ch'eng," the name bestowed by posterity upon a piece of priceless jade disc. The king of Ch'in sought this jade from Chao by promising fifteen cities in exchange, and a clever emissary by the name of Lin Hsiang-ju was able to bring it back from this mission after detecting the King of Ch'in's real intentions of keeping the jade without deeding the fifteen cities to Chao. See *Shih chi*, *chüan* 81.

line 23: Alluding to the title of the 2nd chapter of *Chuang-tzu*. See note to line 8.

line 28: The lines from "a hundred streams" in l. 27 to "laughed at through eternity" in l. 36 are taken almost *verbatim* by Hsin from the opening paragraph of the *Ch'iu-shui* chapter. The corresponding passage in the original, consisting of exactly 100 words, was reduced to Hsin's fifty-seven words which includes six additional words "*ch'ün hsün* (a rhymed-compound meaning "timorously," l. 34), "*ching*" ("in amazement," l. 35), and the three words "*miao-ts'ang-ming*" in l. 32. Legge's translation is as follows (the italics are my own to indicate the words omitted or paraphrased by the poet):

> *The time of the autumnal floods was come*, and the hundred streams were all discharging themselves into the Ho (*i.e.*, the river). Its current was greatly swollen, so that across the channel from bank to bank one could *not distinguish an ox from a horse*. On this the (Spirit-) earl of the Ho laughed with delight, thinking that all the beauty of the world was to be found in his charge. *Along the course of the river he walked east till he came to the North Sea*, over which he looked, with his face to the east, *without being able to see where its waters began. Then he began to turn his face round*, looked across the expanse (as if he were) confronting Jo, and said with a sigh, 'What the vulgar saying expresses about him who has learned a hundred points (of the Tao), and thinks that there is no one equal to himself, was

surely spoken of me. . . . If I had not come to your gate, I should have been in danger (of continuing in my ignorance), and been laughed at for long in the schools of our great System'." (pp. 422-23)

line 33: The three words in this line—*miao ts'ang-ming*—must have been added by the poet in the most deliberate fashion to separate the two long passages of borrowing and adaptation from *Chuang-tzu*. "*Ts'ang-ming*," a compound used in the sense of "ocean," was probably borrowed from Tu Fu, in whose works this phrase occurs five times; *cf.* "*ch'ing (ching)-li-p'o-ts'ang-ming* ("The whale's strength crashes through the ocean's vast expanse") in "*Tseng Han-lin Chang Ssu-hsüeh-shih Chi*," a poem addressed to Chang Chi, *Tu Kung-pu Shih-chi*, *SPPY* edition, *chüan* 9, p. 11b. *Ming*, written without the water radical, and meaning "ocean," also occurs in the first sentence of the first chapter of *Chuang-tzu*, Legge, p. 212.

Wang Yü-ch'eng

THE BAMBOO PAVILION-TOWER OF HUANG-KANG

TRANSLATED BY JAN W. WALLS

INTRODUCTION

REVIEWING the lives of the famous scholar-officials in traditional China, we find that those who valued their integrity most highly were often the ones who enjoyed the least security of office. Their very lives were hinged upon the whim of a despotic sovereign, and many honest and sincere officials found their careers punctuated by periods of exile and disgrace after their honest advice had been either misinterpreted or intentionally misconstrued. Wang Yü-ch'eng was one of these men. His genius won him early favor with his emperor, but his lack of restraint in voicing what he thought to be proper criticism often met with ill favor, and during the last years of his short life, he was forced to pack his baggage nine times—from 988 to 1001: Shang-chou; Chieh-chou; Shan-chou; K'ai-feng; Ch'u-chou; Yang-chou; K'ai-feng; Huang-chou; and Chin-chou.

Wang Yü-ch'eng, sobriquet Yüan-chih, was born in Chü-yeh, Chi-chou, of Shantung Province, north China, in 954. He was of a peasant family, but through his sheer brilliance was able to pass the Imperial Examinations and obtain the highly coveted Advanced Scholar (*chin-shih*) degree in 983. He died from an unknown cause in 1001 at the age of forty-seven. *Chung-kuo Wen-hsüeh-chia Ta-tz'u-tien*, Yang Yin-shen, ed. (Shanghai: Chung Hua Shu Chü, 1939), page 231, gives a detailed biography.

Wang Yü-ch'eng wrote this essay in the year 999, during his exile in Huang-chou. I find it particularly enjoyable because, brief and simple though it is, its descriptive beauty is evident in the first reading, and its surprising depth becomes more and more apparent in subsequent reflection. For only toward the end of his essay does Wang reveal that the Bamboo Pavilion-Tower that he has described so effectively symbolizes the Empire itself; that the simple, frugal, and utilitarian principles governing the structure of the pavilion-tower are precisely those which should govern the motherland. Thereupon his love for the little building becomes love for the ideal world; his scorn for the more exotic edifice mirrors his contempt of the corrupt rule which sends honest men into exile. Reversing the shingles is symbolic of a reversal of administrative policies—a plea to uncover and make use of hidden talents (exiled officials)—and his final resigned optimism toward the future of his pavilion-tower takes on new meaning.

In translating this essay I have tried to retain some of the smoothness and balance of the original; I hope that the many parallel sentences, which are euphonic in Chinese, will not seem tedious in English.

THE BAMBOO PAVILION-TOWER OF HUANG-KANG

The land at Huang-kang produces much bamboo, the greatest stalks of which resemble beams. Bamboo workers split them, cut away their joints, and use them in place of earthen tiles. So it is with every building here; and thus its price is modest and it requires less labor.

At the northwest corner of our city wall the parapet was toppled in ruin, overgrown by thick weeds. There I built a small two-room pavilion-tower that leads to the Moon Wave Pavilion-Tower. In the distance one can imbibe mountain splendor, and on the horizon scoop in river shoals. Deep and still, distant and remote, it defies all description. In summer it is right for enjoying summer showers: there is the roaring sound of cascades; in winter for fine snowfall: there is the tinkling sound of jade. It is right for strumming the zyther: the zyther's tune is harmonious, pleasant; and for chanting poetry: the poem's ring is pure, sublime. It is right for playing *go*: the stones sound click, click; and for playing pitch: the darts sound plunk, plunk. All these effects are enhanced in a pavilion-tower of bamboo.

In times of leisure, when official business subsides, I slip into my swan's-down robe and put on my hermit's cap. Holding in hand the *Book of Changes*, I burn incense, sit in silence, and banish worldly care. Beyond the river and mountains I see only sails in the wind, birds on the sand, misty clouds, bamboo trees, and nothing more. Later, when I awaken from this intoxication, and the steam has vanished from the tea, I bid farewell to the setting sun, and greet the pallid moon: splendid conditions for an exile.

The Cloud Level and Falling Star pavilion-towers were lofty, yes; the Well Crib and Tower of Beauty were magnificent, yes; but they merely housed women of pleasure, concealed song and dance. They are not the concern of a troubled poet; I would not have them.

I have heard the bamboo workers say, "Bamboo can serve as tile for only ten years. If you then reverse the shingles, they will last for twenty years." Alas! In the year 995 I was sent away from the Han Lin Academy to the area of Ch'u; in 996 I was transferred to Kuang-ling; in 997 I entered the Western Office. In 998, on the last day of the year, orders came to go to Ch'i-an. In 999, during the intercalary third month, I arrived here at my district. For four years I have been scurrying about without pause, never knowing where the following year would find me; why should I fear that the Bamboo Pavilion-Tower might waste away? Someone after me, with motives similar to my own, I trust, will adopt and repair it so that this pavilion-tower shall not waste away. (Written on the fifteenth day of the eighth month, 999.)

NOTES

line 1 HUANG-KANG: A city northwest of today's Huang-kang County, Hupei Province.

line 16 PITCH: A game of pitching darts into a pot.

line 27 CLOUD LEVEL: Said to have been built by Han P'u of the Five Dynasties period (A.D. 907–960). Location unknown.

FALLING STAR: Built by Sun Ch'uan, self-proclaimed emperor of the Wu Kingdom (3rd century A.D.). Located forty *li* northwest of Nanking.

line 28 WELL CRIB: Erected by the Han Emperor Wu (141–86 B.C.). It was forty *chang* high, resembling a well crib in shape.

TOWER OF BEAUTY: Erected by Ts'ao Ts'ao (ca. 155–220), King of Wei.

line 34 IN THE YEAR 995: The reign-title of *Chih-Tao*, the second celestial stem *yi*, the eighth horary branch *wei*, which was the year 995.

line 35 HAN LIN ACADEMY: Han Lin literally means "forest of quills." The academy was an exclusive brotherhood of scholar-officials in the capital beginning in the T'ang Dynasty (618–906). Their duties embraced such important functions as the drafting and writing of imperial edicts.

line 36 WESTERN OFFICE: The Western Office of the Imperial Palace housed the Imperial Secretariat. It was entrusted with the drafting of imperial proclamations.

line 38 INTERCALARY THIRD MONTH: An extra month was inserted seven times in nineteen years to make up the deficiency between the solar and lunar years.

line 44 999: The second year of the Hsien-P'ing reign.

Tzu-yeh

SONGS OF THE FOUR SEASONS:
SPRING & SUMMER

TRANSLATED BY MICHAEL WORKMAN

INTRODUCTION

"Tzu-yeh's Songs of the Four Seasons" arose during the Period of Political Division (third to seventh centuries A. D.) among the people of the Wu district near the modern city of Soochow. They are classified as Southern or New Music Bureau poems. These simple love lyrics have exerted a lasting influence on Chinese poetry: most of the traditional love motifs in Chinese literature were perfected in these poems. The "Songs," which were not accompanied by music, followed the form of four regular lines each five words in length.

The poems were popular models for contemporary poets in the Chin and Liu-Sung dynasties (fourth-fifth centuries), and the famous poet Li Po wrote poems in the Tzu-yeh manner. In late T'ang and early Sung times writers of the emergent *t'zu* form of poetry were attracted to these folk poems. The three collections of Tzu-yeh poems (some 124 extant in all) remain important examples of Chinese folk poetry, even though editorial changes by literati are apparent in the poems.

Legend ascribes the authorship of these poems to an individual poetess, Tzu-yeh or Lady Midnight. However a man's viewpoint shows through unmistakably in some poems, and several of the songs are poetic duets (dialogues) between young lovers. But the voice of a feminine persona speaks in the majority of the poems. This unknown poetess seems to embody for the sentimental people of the Wu district the varied personality of love itself.

The emotions of love, heartache, longing, joy, and bitterness dominate these poems. A latent sensual power is implicit in recurrent natural images and in the elaborate punning. Spring wind (love, youth), plum blossoms and swallows (pretty girls), wild geese (friendship and parting), hibiscus flowers (the husband's face), lotus seeds (love play, birth), the bright moon, the north wind, white snow, and cruel frost are emblematic of the variety of human moods. Rusticity and sophistication, scenes of ribaldry, then coquettishness follow one another in pleasing contrast. But the nocturnal lady always returns to her sober thoughts about human life, its transiency, and her own melancholy.

My translations from this collection of seventy-five seasonal poems follow the traditional sequence as transmitted by its compiler, Kuo Mao-ch'ien, in the *Yüeh-fu shih-chi, chüan* 44, *Ssu-pu ts'ung-kan* edition.

TZU-YEH'S SONGS OF THE FOUR SEASONS

SPRING

I
This spring breeze stirs a springtime heart.
And eyes never still to gaze at the mountains
Where forests in shimmering colors abound,
Gay birds pour out their songs in the sun.

II
Green sprouts skirt the length of road.
Red peppers weigh down the purple stalks.
A melodious din at the outskirts of town,
Together we rejoice with spring flowers.

III
Luminous winds flicker in the moon rise.
Once again the woodland is a brocade of flowers.
Lovers frolic under the spring moon,
And bashful maidens trail robes of gauze.

IV
Her enchanted face looks at the view;
The landscape offers its many charms.
When gentle breezes enter the south window,
This lady at the loom cherishes the spring.

V
Before jade pavilions the new moon dims.
Silk dresses cling to the light breeze.
The lure of spring holds back a song,
The cassia wine makes my cheeks shine.

VI
A cuckoo sings behind the bamboos.
Plum blossoms scatter in the roadway.
A beautiful girl* roams under a spring moon.
Her silk skirt trails in fragrant grass.

* Yen-nü also may refer to a girl from Yen in North China.

VII

Bright lights illumine park greenery.
Artemisia glows in the network of stars.
How can I do embroidery in my chamber—
The only woman to shy away from spring!

VIII

Bright clouds glide in brilliant sunlight.
A fragrant breeze scatters forest flowers.
The lovely one paces in the spring park.
Her sash whirls among the flowers.

IX

Thin silk robes cover her reddish sleeves,*
Jade hairpins, moon-shaped earrings.
Let us venture out upon the dew of spring:
To find young men as companions in love.

X

So rich in charm, the blooms in spring forests.
So pitiful, the cries of spring birds.
Spring wind again caressingly
Parts this silken dress of mine.

XI

Young swallows blare out their new tune.
Cuckoos vie in morning racket.
The thrush intent upon its own refrain—
As I rove, easing this spring heart.

XII

Plum flowers all fallen and gone.
Willow catkins are escorted by the wind.
How I lament that in the spring of life
No young man has beckoned me!

XIII

Once parting geese gathered at the sandbar.
Now, nesting swallows greet us in the eave.

* The reference may be to a girl's blushing arms.

Dare we forego a long farewell?
Only if we will meet in spring's brightness!

XIV
Spring garden flowers near yellow.
Ponds from sunshine run green.
We must fill our wine cups to the brim:
Let's tune our strings, end our ditty.

XV
Demurely she lifts her dancing sleeves,
The utter sweep of her weightless shape:
Iridescent these flowers still—
Irreverent spring mood, breeze-bred.

XVI
Splendid, wondrous her dancing air,
She sways in time with the new song.
Her blue dress comes from the gay capital,*
She turns toward me and nods with love.

XVII
Bright moonlight shines on the cassia,
Early blooms, a delicate brocade.
Who could forget him
Or sit alone before a loom?

XVIII
Far rougher times are ahead on this path
Though I've no longer any cares for myself.
Spring breeze rouses the dazzling woodland.
Still I fear the flowers will drop off.

XIX
As I went out to see spring flowers by moonlight,
The magnolia blocked my path.†
Meeting you, how I longed to pluck.
Alas, my hand was deceived.

---

* The capital may be Lo-yang.

† *han-hsiao*, literally, "to smile," can mean the magnolia, "the smiling flower [*han-hsiao-hua*]."

XX

Since I parted from my lover,
The echo of my sigh has never hushed.
Each spring the yellow bud grows.
Its bitter core enlarges day after day.

SUMMER

I

The high hall rises without walls,
Kidnapping winds from every side.
They spread open my lover's silk skirt.
Your glum face breaks into laughter.

II

Toss and turn on luxurious mats.
No need for gauze curtains.
Young man, better not rush in now,
Before I have made myself ready.

III

Early spring began without you, unhappy.
Autumn, winter—still more frozen loneliness.
Playing together in the harsh summer heat,
We share a kindred passion.

IV

Spring goodbyes compare to spring longings.
Summer returns find affection lengthened.
For whom are silk curtains raised?
How much time before I need two pillows?

V

Neatly I set the fan on the bed
And imagine distant winds approach.
Dainty sleeves brush the powdered face—
An elegant lady climbs the tower.*

* It was common for a woman to go to some high place to watch for the return of her beloved.

VI

We shared the taste of delicious cherries;
You offered a fan as a symbol of love.
Touched by your deep devotion,
Within this fragrant chamber, I wait to welcome you.

VII

Though fieldwork and silkworm tasks are over,
An anxious wife has not stopped her chores.
In summer heat she arranges thin robes
To dispatch to her husband far away.

VIII

At dawn I stand on cool roof gardens.
At eve I sleep by the orchid pond.
In moonlight I husband hibiscus flowers.*
Each night I gather the lotus seeds.†

IX

All winds died that hot day
As summer clouds lifted in the dusk.
Hand in hand beneath dense foliage,
We floated melons and sank ripe plums.

X

Vapors arising, this mid-summer's month,
I whistle, walking around the lake.
The lotus has just begun to bear leaves,
Though comely, the flower has not borne seed.‡

XI

Just now I spy him with a green cap—
All spring again has vanished.
The briar thrush has changed its tune.
Among the trees chirp summer crickets.

---

* A pun on *fu-yung*, the hibiscus, which is homonymic with a husband's face.
† "lotus-seed" *(lien)* means "children" *(lien-tzu)*.
‡ Another play on the words for lotus and seed, *cf.* Summer xiv, xv, xx.

XII
The spring peach now ripens.
Spare its blush, I fear your rude hands.
When a flower drops in resplendent summer,
Who will return for its fallen petals?

XIII
When we said goodbye, spring wind was rising.
Summer clouds float in the sky as I come back.
The roads were long, days and months hurried by,
I did not dawdle on purpose.

XIV
Green lotus leaves, a canopy on the pond.
Each lotus flower conceals a ruby crown.
The gentlemen longs to pluck me off.
But my heart yearns for the lotus seed.

XV
Surrounded by a pond of water lilies,
The red hall opens with no inner screens.
Prized bamboo mats and the jade-inlaid bed.
Our union blesses us at will.

XVI
In this fierce summer month
Is there anyone else to fan you?
An elegant lady on the jade terrace,
Inviting your favors in the coolness.

XVII
Spring over, mulberry leaves all gone,
Silkworm tasks of early summer past.
I've plied with thread and spool.
How I wish to tie the knot soon!*

---

* Literally *ch'eng-p'i* means "to complete a roll of cloth," which can be construed to mean "to become a pair or couple." The word for "roll" or "piece" is homonymic with that for "pair."

XVIII
Indeed summer heat is well known,
Here today it's especially hot.
A perfumed kerchief to dust the cool mat;
With him I climb the stairs to rest.

XIX
These scanty clothes too drab.
Even a whirlwind brings no relief.
When will these stifling summer days pass,
So I can amuse you with rouge and powder?

XX
Though humid summer's unfit for excursions,
As multiple cares snarl about me,
I long to sail on the lotus lake
To scatter my thoughts among lotus seeds.

Lao She

NEIGHBORS

TRANSLATED BY WILLIAM A. LYELL, JR.

INTRODUCTION

LAO SHE (1899–1966)[1] is probably best known in this country as the author of *Rickshaw Boy* (*Lo-to Hsiang-tzu*), a novel which became an American best-seller upon the publication of its English translation in 1945. Elements of both native and foreign literary traditions were happily combined in Lao She to produce some of the best Chinese fiction of the first half of the twentieth century. On the one hand he was strongly affected by the English literature he read during his sojourn in London between 1925 and 1930 (Dickens and Conrad were among his favorite authors); and on the other hand he was equally influenced by the tradition of the professional storytellers (*shuo shu te*) whom he so often went to hear in Peking teashops during his youth.

The following story, "Neighbors," reveals traces of both these influences.[2] It also affords us glimpses of city life in China during the early 1930's and is a good example of Lao She, the humorist-raconteur, at his best. In "Neighbors" his humor is aimed at two of his favorite targets: Chinese who gain wealth and prestige through their connections with foreign patrons and young Chinese whose "modern" education has made them so "civilized" that all life and honest feeling have been drained from them. And yet, despite the concentration of satirical barbs, the author is in sympathy with all of his characters. "Neighbors" is an excellent example of Lao She's humor at its warmest. He considered himself primarily a humorist (as distinguished from satirist) by character as well as by profession. He once described the humorist in this way:

> Above all, humor is a frame of mind. We all know people who are overly sensitive and always approach things with a surcharge of emotion, never willing to make allowances for others . . . [Here, of course,

he has the satirist in mind.—*trans*.] A person with a sense of humor is not at all like this . . . he sees the flaws in mankind and wants to point them out to others; however, he does not stop at merely spotting these flaws, but goes on to positively accept them. And thus everyone has something funny about him, the humorist himself being no exception; if we take this to an even higher plane, then the fact that man is limited to a hundred years of life at most and yet would like to live forever, is in and of itself an extremely funny contradiction given in the very nature of human existence. Thus our laughter carries with it an element of sympathy, and at this point humor ceases being merely funny and enters the realm of profundity.³

NOTES

1. In October of 1966 reports from Hong Kong stated that the Red Guards, objecting to Lao She as being "anti-party and anti-Mao," had harrassed him into suicide. (See the article on Lao She by Hsü Chien-wen published serially in the supplement to the *Central Daily News*. Taipei: October 22, 23, & 24, 1966.) The reports have since been verified.

2. "Neighbors / Lin Chü Men" was translated from *A Selection of Lao She / Lao She Hsüan Chi*. Hong Kong: Wen Hüeh Ch'u Pan She, 1961, pp. 75–85.

3. Lao She, *The Rickety Ox-cart / Lao N'iu P'o Ch'e*. Hong Kong: Yü Chou Shu Tien, 1961, pp. 71–72.

LAO SHE / NEIGHBORS

Mrs. Ming was constantly on her guard. To be sure, she had already borne sons and reared daughters for Mr. Ming; and although she was fast approaching forty, she still waved her hair to keep attractive. And yet, in spite of all this, she was still in a state of constant apprehension from morning till night, for she well knew that she had one major flaw: she was illiterate. She felt that she had to do every last thing she could think of to make up for this defect; therefore in looking after her husband and taking care of the children, she was scrupulously diligent. With regard to discipline, however, she had to let the children do pretty much as they pleased, not daring to punish or scold them. She didn't have the nerve to get strict with them, for she was conscious of the fact that because of her illiteracy, her own position was not as high as theirs in the eyes of her spouse. After all, it was only thanks to *him* that she was the mother of such fine children in the first place. In such circumstances, she could not but be constantly on guard. Since her husband was everything to her, she could not afford to strike or scold that husband's children. She was well aware that if her husband really became put out with her he was quite capable of dealing with her in the most humiliating way he could. He could, for instance, take another wife anytime he wanted, and there would be nothing that she could do about it.

She was of a highly suspicious nature, and hence, always felt uneasy in the presence of anything with writing on it. For behind the written word lurked secret meanings which she could never guess. She detested all those housewives and young ladies who knew how to read. However, looking on the brighter side of things, she could console herself with the consideration that her own husband and children were not one whit inferior to all those literate housewives. Furthermore, she had to grant herself that she was naturally bright, enjoyed good fortune, and had a respectable social position. She would never allow others to say that her children were either bad or mischievous, for anything said against the children would constitute an indirect slur on the mother, and she wouldn't stand for that. In everything, she obeyed the wishes of her husband or those of her children. But apart from this hint of subservience, she felt superior to everyone. She availed herself of every opportunity to display her dignity to the servants and neighbors. When her children got into fights with the neighbor's children, she was very likely to join the fray with complete disregard for life and limb, in order to let other people know what a formidable person she was. She had her social position to think of; after all, she was *Mrs. Ming* and her own belligerence reflected the prestige of her husband much as the light of the moon causes people to think of the glory of the sun.

She despised the servants because she felt that they didn't properly respect her. You see, they didn't refer to her as *Madame* Ming every time they opened their mouths; moreover, occasionally they betrayed just the hint of a superior air, making her feel that they were saying to themselves, "Take off that fancy Mandarin dress of yours and underneath we are equals, or maybe you're even more of a humbug than we are." It seemed that the more carefully that she planned something out, the more likely they were to reveal that kind of superior air. This made her long to sink her teeth into them. She often fired servants, for this was the only way that she could spew out some of the excess wrath that welled up inside.

With regard to his wife, Mr. Ming was a despot. However, in such matters as spoiling the children, quarreling with the neighbors, or firing the servants, he did allow her a modicum of freedom. He thought it fitting that in these areas his wife should exercise the prestige of the Ming household. He was a hard-working and proud man. In his heart he himself did not really respect his wife, but neither would he allow outsiders to treat her lightly. For after all, no matter what she was, she was *his* wife. He couldn't take a second wife because he worked for a very wealthy foreigner who was piously religious. A divorce, or the taking of a concubine, would be enough to shatter Mr. Ming's rice bowl.* Since he himself had to muddle along as best he could with such a wife, he would not allow other people to slight her. It was all right for Mr. Ming to beat her, but an outsider wouldn't be permitted to give her so much as a dirty look. Since he was incapable of really loving his wife, he doted to distraction on his children. Everything that he had had to be better than anyone else's and that applied doubly to his own children.

Mr. Ming held his head very high. He provided adequately for his wife, dearly loved his children, and had a money-making occupation. Nor did he have any bad habits. He viewed himself with all the awed respect that one usually reserves for the sages of high antiquity. He had no need to ask favors from people and hence no need to be polite to them. He spent his days at work and in the evenings came home and played with the children. He never read because books

---

* In other words, his pious foreign employer would fire him.

had nothing to offer him; he already knew everything. Whenever he saw a neighbor about to nod to him in greeting, he turned his face away. He had so little respect for his own nation and society that he never gave them a second thought. However, he did have an ideal: to amass enough money to make himself secure and independent as a small mountain.

Yet in spite of all this, he was still somewhat dissatisfied. He told himself that he *should* be happy, but in life there are, it seems, some things that are not entirely subject to one's own regulation and control. Nothing else can take their place. He clearly perceived that there was just such a black spot in him; it was like a tiny foreign object contained within a quartz crystal. Except for this black spot, he was self-confident, even proud; except for this black spot, Mr. Ming was absolutely flawless. Yet there was no way to get rid of that spot, for it grew within his heart.

He knew that his wife was aware of the spot and that it was precisely because of it that she was so given to suspicion. She had done everything possible to erase it, but she realized that it was getting bigger and bigger all the time. At a glance, she was able to judge variations in the spot's size by observing her husband's smiles or the expression in his eyes. But she didn't dare put out her hand to feel it: it was like a black spot on the sun whose intensity is past all imagining. She was afraid that sooner or later someone else was bound to recognize the passionate intensity of her husband's black spot. She had to think of some means of dealing with it.

Now it so happened that Mr. Ming's children were in the habit of stealing his neighbor's grapes. The dividing wall between the two homes was very low, and the children continually clambered over it to make off with the neighbor's plants. The neighbors were a young couple named Yang, and although they were very fond of their garden they never complained of the thefts. Mr. Ming and his wife never actively encouraged the children to go out and steal things, but once they had returned home with the loot, the parents never told them that they were in the wrong. Moreover, they felt that grapes and flowers were not at all like other things and there was nothing so terrible about picking something here and there. As both the Mings saw it, if the children had taken a few flowers and the neighbors had come over to complain about it, then it would really be inexcusable to just ignore the whole matter. But the Yang couple had never come over to complain; Mrs. Ming, in her thinking on the subject, went one step further than her husband and concluded that the Yangs didn't dare come because they were intimidated by the prestige of the Mings. Mr. Ming had long been aware that the Yangs were afraid of him. It wasn't at all because the two young Yangs had in any way openly expressed fear that he knew this, but simply because he felt that everyone ought to be intimidated by a man like himself who always walked with his head held high. Moreover, both the Yangs were teachers, a line of work for which Mr. Ming had never had any respect. He had always felt that teachers were a bunch of paupers without any future prospects.

However, the thing that especially disgusted him about *Mr.* Yang was the fact that *Mrs.* Yang was so very pretty. He had no use for teachers, but women teachers (especially if they were pretty) well, that was something else again. To think that that pauper Yang should have such a wife, ten times better than his own! How could he help but be disgusted? When he thought about it from Mrs. Yang's point of view, he concluded that it was probably a certain lack of foresight that had caused such a smart looking young woman to marry a teacher. Thus there was no real reason for his objecting to Mrs. Yang, but in the end he came to detest her too. Mrs. Ming was aware of all this, for her husband's eyes often roved over in the direction of the short dividing wall between the homes. For this reason she thought it only right that the children should steal the Yang's flowers and grapes; it was a way of punishing that Yang bitch. She had already made up her mind that if that Yang woman ever dared to so much as open her mouth, she'd tear her apart limb by limb.

Mr. Yang was a Chinese of the most up-to-date type who manifested the utmost courtesy in everything he did in order to let people know that he was an educated man. Throughout the affair, he didn't want to say anything about the Ming children's thefts from his garden. It was as though he thought that Mr. and Mrs. Ming—that is, if they were educated people too—would come over and apologize of their own volition. But to pressure them into an apology would smack too much of embarrassing them. But the Mings never once came over on their own to apologize. Mr. Yang didn't dare become angry either, for while the Mings might disregard the rules of etiquette, Mr. Yang had his dignity to preserve.

Yet when the Ming children began to make off with large bunches of his grapes, it was almost more than he could take. It wasn't so much the loss of the grapes that annoyed him, but he did begrudge the time that he had spent on them. He had planted them three years ago and this was the first time that they had borne fruit. The three or four little bunches that had appeared were promptly picked and carried away by the Ming children. Mrs. Yang finally decided to report the whole matter to Mrs. Ming, but Mr. Yang (although he really wanted his wife to go over) held her back; for in the end his concern over the rules of propriety and their status as teachers was strong enough to overcome his anger.

Mrs. Yang didn't see it that way at all, however; she simply had to go over, and moreover, she would go in an attitude of plenary courtesy; she had no intention of getting into an argument or fight. Mr. Yang, fearing that his wife would consider him a jellyfish, could not very well insist on her not going. Thus it was that Mrs. Yang and Mrs. Ming finally met.

Mrs. Yang was very polite: "Mrs. Ming, I presume? My own surname is Yang."

Mrs. Ming knew exactly what it was that Mrs. Yang had come for, and she detested her from the bottom of her heart. "Uh huh, I've known your name for a long time."

The education that Mrs. Yang had received caused her to blush at the brusqueness of her reply, but she couldn't think of anything to say. Yet she had to say something. "It's really nothing. The children . . . It really doesn't matter, but they have taken a few grapes."

"You don't say?" Mrs. Ming's tone was sweetly musical. "Children just love grapes. Grapes are fun. Of course, I would never let them *eat* them. They just take them for fun."

"Our grapes," gradually the red began to recede from Mrs. Yang's face, "are not easy to grow. It was three whole years before they bore fruit."

"But it's your grapes that I'm talking about; they're so sour that I won't allow the children to eat them, but I do let them play with them. What a paltry vine you have, so few grapes on it!"

"Now as for children," Mrs. Yang began, remembering some of the educational theory that she had learned in school, "all children are mischievous, but Mr. Yang and I *are* very fond of plants."

"Mr. Ming and I are very fond of them too."

"What if your plants were stolen by the neighbor's children?"

"Who would dare to steal *our's*?"

"And if your own children steal other people's?"

"They've stolen yours. Is that what you're trying to say? Then the best thing to do is to move away and not live here anymore. You see, our kids are very fond of playing with grapes."

There was nothing else that Mrs. Yang could say, and lips trembling with anger, she went home. Upon running into her husband, she almost burst into tears.

Mr. Yang reasoned with his wife at great length. Although he felt that Mrs. Ming was in the wrong, he didn't contemplate any further action. He felt that Mrs. Ming was barbaric and to wrangle with a barbarian would demean one's social status. But his wife wasn't willing to let it go at that and insisted that he seek vengeance on her behalf. He thought it all over, at great length, and finally it dawned upon him that Mr. Ming couldn't possibly be as barbaric as his wife. He'd negotiate with the husband. He'd write a letter. He'd write an exceedingly polite letter, not mentioning the last round between his own wife and Mrs. Ming. Nor would he say that he thought the children had been misbehaving. He would simply implore Mr. Ming to order his children not to come and wreak havoc on his plants anymore. In this way he felt that he'd be acting the part of an educated man. He thought of such high-sounding phrases as "the amity that exists between close neighbors . . . infinitely thankful . . . will be extremely appreciated." In his mind's eye he saw Mr. Ming receiving the letter, being moved by its contents, and coming over in person to apologize. With a feeling of utter satisfaction he drew to a close a letter of no inconsiderable length and asked the maid to take it over to the Ming household.

After Mrs. Ming had scared her neighbor back to her own nest, she felt particularly pleased with herself. For a long time she had been itching to lay into a woman like Mrs. Yang, and the latter had finally afforded her an opportunity. She began imagining to herself the way that Mrs. Yang would probably explain the matter to her husband and how the two of them together would see the folly of their conduct. Even if it is wrong for children to steal grapes, still one ought to consider whose children they are. When the Ming children steal grapes, one ought not feel resentful. Upon realizing this basic principle, the Yang family would undoubtedly stand totally in awe of the Mings. Mrs. Ming couldn't help feeling very happy.

When the Yangs' maid brought the letter over, Mrs. Ming was filled with suspicion. Obviously the letter had been written to Mr. Ming by that Yang woman with the intention of wiping her out. She hated the written word. Even more, she hated that Yang trollop who was able to write such words. She decided not to accept the letter. Although she was quite assured of her husband's love for the children, still she had to bear in mind that the letter was written by that Yang woman. Perhaps because of the prestige that the trollop enjoyed in her husband's eyes, he might even go so far as to give her a beating. If her husband really did give her a beating and that Yang baggage heard of it, that would really be too much to take. To be beaten for something else would be all right, but to be beaten for that Yang woman . . . she'd have to make preparations. When her husband arrived home she'd lay the foundation—she'd say that the Yang family had come over and started a big row over a few sour old grapes; she'd tell him that they had threatened to write him a letter demanding an apology. Hearing all this, her husband would certainly refuse to accept the letter and then the victory would be totally hers.

While waiting for her husband to arrive home, she composed what she'd say to him and even found ways of sandwiching in all of her husband's favorite phrases. And Mrs. Ming's words did indeed stir up the ardor of his love for his children. He might have been able to excuse *Mrs.* Yang had she not said that his children were bad. But now she had called forth his positive contempt. To think that she had given her hand in marriage to a poor disgusting teacher like Mr. Yang! She certainly couldn't be a very good piece of goods herself. By the time that Mrs. Ming's narration reached the point where she reported that the Yangs intended to send a letter demanding an apology, Mr. Ming was really boiling. He was thoroughly disgusted with literary paupers like Yang who would immediately resort to the writing brush over absolutely nothing. Working for a foreigner, Mr. Ming was convinced that only a signature on a typewritten contract carried any weight at all. He couldn't possibly imagine of what use a hand-written letter from a poor teacher might be. Yes, if the Yangs sent the letter back over, he'd refuse to accept it.

And yet that black spot in his heart caused him to be curious about what Mrs. Yang's writing might look like. Writing was worthless in itself, but then one had to take into consideration whose writing it was. Mrs. Ming had foreseen such an eventuality early in the game: she said that the letter was written by Mr. Yang. Of course Mr. Ming had no time to waste on a stinking letter written by that disgusting Yang bum. He was firmly convinced that a letter from even the very highest of Chinese officials did not carry the weight of the signature of a foreigner.

Mrs. Ming sent the children to lie in wait at the door with firm instructions not to accept any letter from the Yangs. She, herself, certainly had no time to waste in watching the Yang home. She was quite pleased with her own success, and although one would have thought that she'd let it go at that, she kept thinking of other steps to take and even went so far as to suggest that her husband buy the house that the Yangs were living in. Mr. Ming knew that he didn't have the spare cash to buy a house, but he agreed anyway. Just listening to his wife speak of such a plan was music to his ears. It was too good to pass up. No matter whether the Yangs owned the house or were renting, he'd think of some way to get hold of it, and then he'd sell it right out from under them! It did his heart good to hear his children say, "We're going to buy that house over there," for outright purchase was the greatest of all possible victories. Houses, cars, things of gold—whenever he thought of buying such things he always became increasingly aware of his own greatness.

Even though he considered the Mings' refusal to accept his letter as a personal insult, Mr. Yang did not favor sending the letter back over again. For a while he thought of having it out with Mr. Ming, once and for all, right out in the street, but it was just a thought. His social position, you understand, would not allow him to resort to such barbaric behavior. He was reduced to weakly explaining to his wife what rotten eggs the Mings were and how there wouldn't be much point in starting a fight with rotten eggs. With this he was able to comfort himself to some extent.

Mrs. Yang did not give vent to her anger either; nor was she able to come up with any good plan for revenge. She began to think that "to be civilized" meant always taking the short end of the stick. She expressed a number of pessimistic views and insights on the subject to her husband and saying such things straight out helped her to get rid of quite a bit of her own spleen. The two of them were in the midst of babbling away their anger in this fashion when the maid brought in a letter. Mr. Yang took a look at the envelope: the street number was right, but it was addressed to Mr. Ming. For a moment he thought of keeping the letter, but he immediately realized that that was something that an upright man really couldn't do. He told the maid to take the letter over to the Mings.

Despite her previous resolution, Mrs. Ming had in fact been spying on the Yang house for a long time, and upon seeing the Yang maid approach with the letter, she began to fear that the children stationed at the door might not really know how to handle the situation. Thus she steeled herself for action and personally joined the fray.

"Take it back, we don't want to even look at it."

"It's for Mr. Ming," the maid said.

"I know, but the head of this household doesn't have the time to waste reading your letter." Mrs. Ming was extremely decisive.

The maid handed the letter to her saying, "It was mailed to the wrong address. It's not ours."

"Oh, sent to the wrong address was it?" Mrs. Ming rolled her eyes around in confusion for a moment. She had it! "Let the master of your house receive it! Do you think that I can't read? Don't try to put anything over on me!" Slam! ! The door closed.

To the consternation of Mr. Yang, the maid brought the letter back. He didn't want to go back over with the letter himself, nor was he willing to open it up to see what was inside. At the same time he really felt that Mr. Ming was a rotten egg too—for he knew that Mr. Ming had by now returned home and had formed a united front with that barbaric wife of his. How ought he handle the business of the letter? To confiscate another man's letter would certainly be less than honorable. After thinking over a number of possibilities, he finally decided that he would put it in another envelope, address it correctly, and toss it into the nearest mailbox the very next morning. After he had stuck a penny stamp on the envelope, he was even able to smile.

The next morning the Yangs were so pressed for time in getting to school that he forgot the letter. It was only after arriving at work that he remembered it, but then it was too late to go back after it. Fortunately, he remembered that the letter had come by regular delivery and therefore, he decided, it couldn't have been anything very important. It certainly wouldn't make any difference if he sent it out a day late.

When he got home from school he didn't feel like going out again and stuck the letter in one of his school books, promising himself that he'd be certain to mail it out the very next morning. Having thus disposed of the matter, he was just about to sit down to supper when he heard a great commotion over at the Mings'. Mr. Ming himself was a fastidious man and would never demean himself by screaming or shouting while beating his wife, but Mrs. Ming, the recipient of the beatings, was not at all that fussy about preserving such niceties. She wailed and howled for all she was worth so that even the children were attracted by the fuss. Mr. Yang listened very carefully, but he couldn't make out what it was all about. Suddenly he thought of the letter; maybe it was important. Perhaps because he hadn't received the letter on time some affair or other had miscarried and now he was taking it out on his wife. This thought made him very uncomfortable. He thought of opening the letter to see what was inside, but he didn't have the nerve. Yet by not looking at the letter he managed to so frustrate himself that he couldn't even enjoy his evening meal.

After supper the Yang family's maid ran into the Mings' maid. A falling out of employers doesn't do any harm to the friendship between servants; the Mings' maid let the cat out of the bag. Mr. Ming had beaten his wife over a letter, a very important letter. After the Yang maid had returned and reported this intelligence, Mr. Yang wasn't able to sleep. He was sure that the letter in question must be the one that he had. But if it really were an important letter, why hadn't it been sent by registered mail? Moreover, why had the sender been so careless as to write down the wrong street number? He thought about this for a long while and the only conclusion that he was able to reach was that businessmen are very careless with regard to the written word; this was probably sufficient to explain the mistaken address. Add to that the fact that Mr. Ming didn't ordinarily write or receive many letters and one could very well see how the postman might have simply looked at the street number without noticing the name. Perhaps he didn't even remember that there was a Ming family on the street.

Such thoughts as these caused Mr. Yang to become aware of his own superiority. After all, Mr. Ming was just a rotten egg whose only talent was raking in money. But if Mr. Ming was a rotten egg to begin with, then why couldn't Mr. Yang open up the letter and take a peek? To be sure, reading another man's mail was a legal offense, but a man like Mr. Ming wouldn't be aware of that anyway.

But what if Mr. Ming should come over and demand the letter back? No, it wasn't a good idea to open it. He picked up the letter a good many times, but in the end he lacked the nerve to open it. At the same time he no longer felt like sending it over to Mr. Ming. If it really were an important letter, then in the hands of Mr. Yang it might prove very useful. Of course this was not open and above board, but then who told Mr. Ming to be such a rotten egg? Who told him to deliberately give the Yangs a hard time? Rotten eggs ought to be punished. He began thinking of his grapes.

Then he started reconsidering things all over again. He thought; he pondered; and in the end he changed his mind again. He would still send the letter to Mr. Ming the very next day. Furthermore, he would send out his own letter exhorting the Mings to look to the conduct of their children. He'd show that rotten egg of a Ming how courteous and amiable a really educated man could be. He had no hopes of reforming Mr. Ming, but at least he could make him realize that teachers are *gentlemen,* and that would be enough.

Mr. Ming ordered his wife to go over and demand the letter back. He already knew its contents for he had bumped into the man who had written it and had already taken the proper precautions that the misplaced letter had indicated. But he still didn't want the letter to remain in the hands of the disgusting bum of a Yang. The heart of the matter was this: he and a friend had used the name of his foreign employer to smuggle some goods into the country and somehow or other that rich and piously religious foreign employer had gotten wind of it. The letter was, in effect, a warning from his friend advising him to find some way of pulling the wool over the eyes of the foreigner.

It was not at all the case that Mr. Ming was afraid that the Yangs might make public the contents of the letter, for in his heart he had no respect for his own government and he had never feared Chinese law. Even if his compatriots did find out that he had been engaged in smuggling, it still wouldn't matter very much. What he was really afraid of was that the Yangs might mail the letter off to the foreigner and thus prove that he had, in fact, been guilty of smuggling. He thought that that disgusting Mr. Yang was just the kind of devious person who might peek into the letter and then go on to foul things up for him. He, himself, couldn't very well go to get the letter back, for if he met that Yang bastard face to face, there'd certainly be a fight. From the bottom of his heart he was thoroughly disgusted with guys like Yang. He had always felt that that Yang guy deserved a good working over. But in the end, it was his wife whom he sent after the letter. After all, it was because she had refused to accept it that such a fuss had been stirred up in the first place, and this was a good way of punishing her.

Mrs. Ming really didn't want to go over because it would be simply too embarrassing. She'd rather take another beating from her husband than to go over and lose face at the Yangs'. She procrastinated until her husband had gone to work and then spied on the Yangs until she had satisfied herself that they had gone to work too. Finally she sent her maid over to arrange the whole thing through the Yangs' maid.

Mr. Ming was called on the carpet by the foreigner and subjected to an interrogation. Fortunately since he had already seen the friend who had written the misaddressed letter, he was well prepared for what was coming. He was able to cover up everything very well during the interrogation, but he was still uneasy about the letter. The hardest thing to take was the fact that such a letter had to fall into the hands of nobody else but that disgusting pauper of a Yang! He just had to think of a way of punishing the rascal.

After arriving home, his first words were to ask his wife if she had gotten the letter back. Mrs. Ming, was, as ever, on her guard. She told her husband that the Yangs had refused to give the letter back and that took the responsibility for the mistake off her own shoulders. Hence Mr. Ming's anger was diffused over a great number of people rather than being concentrated on her. It simply seemed a case of a disgusting pauper of a teacher daring to cross the great Mr. Ming. So that's the way things stood!! He ordered his children to climb over the dividing wall and stamp down every single plant in the Yangs' yard. Then they were to report back to him and he'd consider what further steps he might take. The children were beside themselves for joy and spared not a single plant within reach.

After the children had returned from their "mission to the frontiers," the postman made the delivery that usually comes somewhat after four in the afternoon. After Mr. Ming had read the two letters, it was difficult to tell whether he felt sorrow or happiness. The misaddressed letter made him happy: he realized that Yang had not, after all, opened and read it. But that letter that Mr. Yang had written made him feel really mad, made him even more disgusted with that bastard pauper. He felt that only a pauper like Yang would ever be capable of that degree of politeness. Just to think that a man could be polite to such a revolting degree! He was glad that he had had his children smash down all their plants and flowers.

On the way home, Mr. Yang felt very good. He had expressed his original intentions in his letter and had, moreover, exhorted a neighbor to goodness; this sort of thing would certainly be enough to reform Mr. Ming to the path of righteousness. Upon arriving home, he was utterly stunned! The plants in his backyard looked as though they had been dumped there by a garbage truck. The entire yard was in a state of chaos. He had no doubts about who had done this to him, but what could he do? He tried to collect himself so that he might objectively consider his next move. After all it wouldn't do for an educated man to react emotionally to such a shock. Try as he would, though, he was no longer capable of being objective. That tiny drop of barbarian blood that was left in him after so much education began to boil up, and made dispassionate thought impossible.

He ripped off his coat and began gathering up pieces of brick. He took careful aim across the wall at the windows in the Ming house and began throwing. The sound of breaking glass was a symphony to his ears. He wasn't conscious of anything anymore, except his own joy, his own sense of fulfillment, and even a feeling of glory! It was as though a civilized man had suddenly become a barbarian. He began to be conscious of his own strength, of his own guts. He felt the way that he felt when he stood naked just after a bath, completely free and unrestrained, a new man. He felt young, ardent, free, and brave.

When he had smashed almost all the windows within reach, he went back to his room to rest. He waited for Mr. Ming to come over and fight him; he wasn't afraid. He puffed wildly on a cigarette and looked for all the world like a victorious warrior. He waited for a long time, but there wasn't even the slightest stir from the direction of the Mings'.

Mr. Ming had no intention of going over to the Yangs', for he felt now that Mr. Yang wasn't really all that disgusting after all. Looking around at the broken glass, although he wasn't pleased by it, he wasn't altogether pained either. He even began considering the possibility of enjoining the children from making off with the Yangs' flowers and grapes after this; previously, nothing had been able to move him to think in this direction. But the broken shards of glass changed his mind. As he thought things over, Mrs. Yang's image flashed before his eyes, and thinking of her, he could not but hate *Mr.* Yang. But now he realized that there was a difference between "hate" and "disgust." "Hate" carried with it a slight hint of respect.

The next day was Sunday. Mr. Yang was in the yard cleaning up his garden. Mr. Ming was inside his house repairing the windows. It seemed as though the whole world were at peace and mutual understanding had finally come to mankind.

Wang Kai

FROM THE MUSTARD SEED GARDEN MANUAL OF PAINTING

TRANSLATED BY HENRY W. WELLS

INTRODUCTION

SINCE the procedure in the following verses is by no means common, and may possibly be viewed with suspicion or even thought eccentric, the translator may be allowed a few comments by way of apology. This brief anthology renders into English verse passages from the well-known guide to Chinese art, *The Mustard Seed Garden Manual of Painting*, compiled by Wang Kai and his associates, and first published in 1701. "Rendered" would, perhaps, be a more fitting word than "translated," for these versions are undeniably free; but it is hoped that they are nonetheless essentially faithful to the meaning of the Chinese and at least not licentious from the literary point of view. The reader may well ask, to begin with, why render prose as verse? The question calls for comments on several of the broader issues at stake.

Among the innumerable fine arts assiduously cultivated by the Chinese through nearly two millennia, picture-making enjoyed the highest prestige, standing beside music and writing as virtually an essential accomplishment of "the complete gentleman." Painting also engaged the efforts of professionals—as a class viewed at times rather superciliously by the amateurs—who were scholars, gentlemen, and frequently officials. Any commanding view of Chinese civilization requires close attention to the high status of pictorial art, the supreme discipline of the eye.

It must be acknowledged that literature occupies an unrivalled position from the strategic point of view. Within the trinity of major activities in the aesthetic life it stood in the center, music on one hand, painting on the other. The three arts were most intimately interrelated, each closely associated with the others. Thus poetry, which was held to be the finest flower of imaginative literature, was, of course, frequently sung, chanted or performed with instrumental accompaniment. Similarly, writing in various ways accompanied painting. Many pictures are attended by poems written beside them. More important, Chinese painting is intensely literary, just as much poetry is highly pictorial or descriptive. Painters are inspired by much the same sentiments and ideas as the writers. The subject-matter in the two arts clearly has much in common, both in terms of philosophy and of actual images. Moreover, a highly conscious and deliberate approach to all the arts produced an immense literature on painting from the Han Dynasty through the Ch'ing, equal in quantity and quality to that on literature and poetics. The scholar's grasp of imaginative literature was greatly strengthened by his knowledge of the literature on painting just as his grasp of painting was strengthened by his knowledge of poetry and its critics.

The following verses are offered as a somewhat unusual gesture in support of these familiar observations. The writer hopes that they indicate anew how much that is essentially poetic resides in the literature on painting and how closely in Chinese ways of thinking the two arts are allied. The general topic may be considered from many angles. Here the approach is uncommon. Passages from one of the most famous critical works on painting are rendered in English verse.

So that the translator may at least stand frankly in open view, the source is, as already stated, an easily accessible book, *The Chih Tzu Yüan*, or *Mustard Seed Garden Manual of Painting*, compiled by the seventeenth-century scholar, Wang Kai, assisted by Wang Shih and Wang Nieh and others. The work is eclectic in every sense of the word. It appeared in successive volumes over a period of several years. Its authors looked backward through the centuries in creating their commentary and in selecting their copious illustrations. Many schools of painting are represented. For over two centuries this became the most popular manual on the subject. It has been reprinted and republished many times. A marked distinction must be drawn between the publications giving the illustrations in wood-block cuts and those presenting them as brush work. The first printed edition using lithographic process and hence reproducing early hand-painted editions was published in Shanghai, 1887. The Bollingen Series has produced a superb facsimile. An abridgment in popular form includes an extensive Introduction by Mai-mai Sze.

The manual is both practical and theoretical, telling one how to mix paints and clarify thoughts. Chinese scholars at first tended to view it as popular and hence in some sense vulgar, a text for beginners, in short, a colossal handbook. Recently it has been more seriously regarded in its own country and widely consulted abroad. Fine copies are in many libraries and museums; to mention but one, an admirable example in the Nelson-Atkins Museum, Kansas City. The commentary deals with many types of subject-matter and problems in technique; among the areas conspicuously represented are landscape painting, trees, rocks, people, flowers, grasses, insects, birds, and beasts.

In testing the validity of my general thesis, I have compiled a considerable anthology of verses based on this and similar books; for example, from *The Chinese on the Art of Painting*, by Osvald Siren, I have versified over eighty passages to exemplify the poetic value of the original commentaries, while I have found well over a score of passages in *The Mustard Seed Garden Manual* inviting, as I thought, such treatment. Landscape is the outstanding topic but commentaries on flower and animal painting are often of considerable poetic value. Especially in the commentaries on the representation of persons, animals, and birds, even the important role of humor in Chinese painting is well illustrated. Rarely does Chinese descriptive prose rise to such distinguished heights.

In general it may be said that the Chinese do not write poems "about" paintings, as the Europeans have often done (witness Rilke and Browning) but write in a highly poetic manner on the identical subjects chosen by poets and painters and on the common grounds of their approach to art. It will be recalled that during the baroque period in Europe poems with titles such as "Advice to a Painter" were in vogue. These verses seem relatively prosaic when placed beside the analogous Chinese prose. It may also be worth mention that some of the Chinese commentaries, even in *The Mustard Seed Garden Manual* itself, are in verse, presumably to help beginners to memorize the good advice given them.

The following are a few books dealing in various ways with these matters: *Li Tai Ming Hua Chih* [Notes on Famous Painters of All Dynasties], 1922; Shio Sakanishi, *The Spirit of the Brush*, 2 vols., 1933; Osvald Siren, *The Chinese on the Art of Painting*, Peiping, 1936, New York, 1963; A. C. Soper, a translation of Kuo Jo-hsu's *Experiences in Painting*, American Council of Learned Societies, Studies in Chinese and Related Civilizations, 6, 1951; Jan Tschichold (ed), *Chinese Color Prints from The Mustard Seed Garden Manual of Painting*, 1952; Wang Shih-chen (ed.), *Wang Shih Hua Yüan*, Collected Writings on Painting, Preface 1590, facsimile 1922.

WANG KAI / FROM THE MUSTARD SEED GARDEN MANUAL OF PAINTING
[1679]

The character of trees lies in their roots.
When growing in the mountain forests, full
With deepest undergrowth, the roots are hid,
Mysterious, more than ever wonderful,
Stretching to unconscionable length,
Clinging with inviolable strength.

Trees that grow among the fallen rocks
Or those whose roots are washed by forest springs
Or cling to cliffs precipitous and steep
Have roots exposed that brave what winter brings.
They are like aged hermits gnarled and lean
Whose purity remains forever green.

In painting trees in groups it will be best
To make distinctions in the ways they grow,
Especially attending to their roots,
Knotted, gnarled and venerable, so
That all have character, not like a saw
With rows of teeth but souls evoking awe.

•

Pine trees are like men with noble minds
Whose quiet manner shows their hidden powers,
Like dragons coiled inside a misted gorge
Thriving equally in sun or showers.
They allure us more than other trees,
Yet none evokes such holy awe as these.

Pines should be painted with a look of iron,
Strong and irresistible yet kind
In heart, their needles soft as new-spun silk,
Their trunks well armored with a stubborn rind.
If you approach them with an awe-filled soul
Your painting speedily must reach its goal.

•

Spirit is no less basic than man's flesh,
Determining his manner and his feature.
Rocks are the roots of clouds, the pith of earth,
No less alive than any living creature.
The slightest thought of any lifeless rock
Must give the cultivated soul a shock.

Rocks without vivifying souls are dead,
Mere dry and dusty bones, not worth a thought.
What painter would so paint them if he knew
The Universal Spirit as he ought?
Many are the ways that painters strive
To picture rocks. Think this: rocks are alive!

•

A range of mountains with a single peak
Above the rest denotes a social scene.
The monarch gathers to his noble breast
His courtiers, his counselors and queen,
Embracing all as each had been his guest.
Thus is perfect harmony expressed.

Another mountain is the emperor
Seated solitary and alone
Close to the sky. Above mankind he broods
In perfect solitude upon his throne.
Wang Wei in representing this was wise,
Deep in clear thought, one with the clouds and skies.

Rocks are the bones of mountains; waterfalls
Carve out the rocks. Some say, water is weak
But I say that all such are thoughtless men
Not knowing what they think or glibly speak.
Water holds the mountains in its thrall.
Chiao Kung declared it to be structural.

Is not water which is always flowing,
Trickling, splashing, foaming from its birth—
Whether in rushing rivers or the ocean—

Life-blood and marrow of the Heavens and Earth?
Blood nurses embryos and marrow, bones.
Who believes the earth composed of lifeless stones?

Marrowless bones are actually dust.
Mountains are living sinews, lords of all.
Since the ancients knew how mountains grow
They paid deep reverence to each waterfall.
Huang Kung-wang excelled in this demesne.
None better painted this most moving scene.

Wang Wei declared: in drawing waterfalls
Use many interruptions but no break;
Leave intervals within the rapid flow;
Where the brush stops your fancy must awake.
Thus a dragon, lord of sky-born powers,
Unites his tail and head in watery showers.

•

Clouds are the ornaments of earth and sky,
Embroidery of mountains, lakes and streams.
We hear them smite the mountains with such force
That thunder bellows and livid lightning gleams.
Such is the nature and the power of clouds,
Veiling the highest summits in their shrouds.

•

People in pictures are an audience
The landscape summons to enjoy the view,
Hinting at new pleasures and fresh thoughts
Interchanged between the scene and you.
Many animate figures there must be,
All paying tribute to the scenery.

These people should be drawn in moderate size,
Never elaborated in detail,
Turning vain attention to themselves;
Always the spell of the landscape should prevail.
Painters who observe a different course
Must find their pictures lacking aim and force.

A figure should be seen who contemplates
The mountain, while the mountain bends to him;
A player of the lute applauds the moon
Whose gracious radiance floods his face and limb.
There must be continuity in all,
Nature and man in thoughts reciprocal.

·

Mountains in the distance should be graced
With towers or tall pagodas since so far
The mountains stand no figure can be seen.
Men and mountains in interaction are
The very essence of the Heavens and Earth,
From whose conjunction wisdom comes to birth.

The temple in the mountains is the sign
That man and Heaven actually are one.
Its graceful turret rises to the stars,
Minute itself though through it peace is won.
When hills gain grandeur and vitality
The viewer's soul soars to Infinity.

Meaning ever must exceed the view,
Vision be within and not without.
So from the speck of this pagoda flows
An effluence like an echo tossed about
Between the hills. The far pagoda's bell
Assures the painter he has painted well.

·

To paint a flower learn first to paint the bud
And this at its beginning, middle, end.
A bud half opened shows its tough peduncle
In profile on which all the petals depend.
When buds are opening from the green leaves' husk
The flower is born full of its fragrant musk.

Issuing from its shroud it first extends
A single petal like a small bird's tongue
Sipping nectar from a new-born flower,
Prelusive to the later petal throng,

Or like a finger issuing from a hand
That still is closed, saluting spring's command.

Color appears first, the merest tint;
Lastly comes the fragrance of the flower,
Each like a pearl, each painted separately
In homage to the beauty of its hour.
Each is a star alighted on a stem,
Glory of a fleeting diadem.

To paint a bud first paint the hard peduncle,
Although each flower is different, yet the same
Form appears in each of these green wombs
Out of which leaps forth the blossom's flame.
Chrysanthemum alone of flowers receives
Its birth from what seems layers of young leaves.

Different as the myriad blooms may be,
The essential form lies in this tough, round ball.
Variants are trivial, for the strength
Of the chrysanthemum is gathered all
Together in this quintessential form
Which painters should examine as their norm.

·

In painting most things paint the head the first
But painting butterflies first paint the wings.
The divine spirit harbors most in them,
The most celestial of aerial things.
In flight the heavenly wings provide a screen
For half the body; at rest the whole is seen.

The head has two antennae while between
A tubular mouth draws nectar. When in flight
This is withdrawn. The wings are stretched at dawn
But folded in the quiet hours of night.
It flutters among flowers, brightly arrayed,
Suggesting some fine lady with her maid.

·

Although the praying mantis may be small
It should be painted with true majesty,
Much like a tiger leaping on its prey,
Its two eyes flaming with ferocity.
Such rabid creatures have a true repute
In art, as war-songs on a peaceful lute.

·

To paint a bird first fix the upper part
That marks that section of the creature's beak;
Then sketch the upper of the lower half;
Finish that portion with a lusty streak.
Dot in the eye to center and behind,
Then have head, neck and upper body lined.

Proceed next to the breast and all below,
Curving stomach, sharply pointed tail;
Shade in the wings, as capable of flight;
Then, at the last, sketch lightly without fail
Each crocked, clinging claw and slender leg:
The whole should bear the aspect of an egg.

SEVEN TALES OF YAMATO

TRANSLATED BY GERALD B. MATHIAS

INTRODUCTION

THE *Yamato-monogatari*, Yamato tales (Yamato is an ancient name for Japan), is one of a mere handful of prose works surviving from before the turn of the millennium; it dates from the middle of the tenth century, about the time that classical Japanese culture was reaching its peak.

For a few hundred years the Japanese elite had been enthusiastically importing and adapting the culture of China. Everything, from styles of clothing, art, and architecture to religion and political structure, was imported and modified to fit the traditional values or the more limited economic means of the Japanese. But most important of all the new elements to the scriptless nation was the Chinese written language.

Although the individual symbols of the Chinese script stand for words or morphemes rather than sounds (much as we use 4 for "four" but not for "for"), the Japanese soon learned to make phonetic use of the characters (as if 4 were used for "four," "for," and "fore") for the transcription of untranslatable proper nouns and so forth. In other words, they developed a native script which they might freely have used to write in their native tongue. Unfortunately the conviction that the Chinese language was the only proper one for serious writing had taken firm root even more quickly. Virtually all artistic or scholarly writing was done in Chinese, and the ability to read and write Chinese was the minimum criterion of an educated man.

Only in the *waka*, the native poetic form, was the sound of the Japanese language revered and allowed to develop. The *waka* was an essential part of Japanese culture. The form consisted of five lines of five, seven, five, seven, and seven syllables respectively. The cultured Japanese used the delicacy, the euphemism, and the discipline of the *waka* in every kind of communication, from courtship to consolatory messages. An exceptionally skillful creation by a sensitive person was an object to be recorded and cherished, and many collections of *waka* of this period are extant.

Native language prose was a different matter. Although a large amount of prose fiction is known to have been in circulation by the tenth century, it was not esteemed as literature, but considered frivolous women's stuff. It was not valued enough to make it worth recopying faster than the originals wore out or were lost, and almost none of it survives. The *Yamato-monogatari* owes its survival largely to the honor it pays the *waka*, since more than anything else it serves to place the *waka* in the context of the events that occasioned their creation.

The standard text of the *Yamato-monogatari* comprises 173 tales, according to the accepted enumeration (in the oldest texts there is no formal separation of one tale from the next). The majority are probably based on fact, for the *dramatis personae* are largely identifiable historical persons, and most of them were contemporaries of the unknown compiler of the tales.

Perhaps two-thirds of the tales are but short anecodtes with *waka* as punch-lines, while the rest, many of which seem to be of oral tradition, are more story-like in length and plot. I have chosen seven of the relatively story-like tales for translation here. However, the purpose of the tales was not so much to relate events as to hint at the delight or pathos evoked in the aesthetically sensitive person by the events or situations depicted, and the endings may seem flat or anti-climactic to the modern reader.

My translation of the prose tends to be literal, with two general exceptions. Where literal translation might raise questions that have no bearing on the story, the translation has been simplified. Thus *seusyau* "Lesser Captain" is rendered "Captain" to obviate explanation of the rank system. Where annotation is essential, it has been blended into the text unmarked. For example, "Ono no Komachi" is expanded to "Ono no Komachi, the famed beauty and poet." As for the poems, which are as complex as they are brief, a full exegesis would be inordinately lengthy and literal translation is impossible; they have accordingly been paraphrased in a prose compromise between what the poem says and what it means, with occasional bracketed notes. The originals are provided in a transliteration of the ancient spelling; Italian values for the vowels and English values for the consonants result in a rough approximation of what is believed to have been the pronunciation of the period.

The text translated is that edited by Abe Toshiko and Imai Gen'ei in *Nippon koten bungaku taikei,* vol. 9 (Tokyo: Iwanami shoten, 1961), pp. 216–398.

(27) A person called Kaishō became a Buddhist priest. There was no one there to do his laundry while he was living on the mountain, and so he used to send it to his parents. Once when they became disgruntled (what can have occasioned it?) and asked, "How can a person who becomes a priest against the advice of his parents and brothers make such annoying demands of them?" Kaishō wrote this poem and sent it to them:

> ima fa ware   And now where might I go?
> iduti yukamasi   Even on this holy mountain
> yama nite mo   the melancholy affairs
> yo no uki koto fa   of the world do not cease to
> nafo mo taenu ka   plague me.

(103) Heichū, at the height of his amorousness, went to the market place. (In those days noble persons went to the market in pursuit of amorous pleasures.) And it was a day when the Ladies in the service of the late Consort were out to market. Heichū set to flirting with them and he fell in love as never before. Afterwards he sent a letter. The women sent back to ask whom the letter was for, as there had been many in the carriage. Therefore the man said:

> momosiki no   Though I saw a number of
> tamoto no kazu fa   courtly sleeves, the
> misikadomo   crimson ones in particular
> wakite omofi no   aroused my longing.
> iro zo kofisiki

This meant the daughter of the Governor of Musashi. She was the one who had been wearing a very deeply colored red silk garment. It was she who was the object of his fancy. And so it was this Musashi who answered his letter and whom he won over. Fair of features and long haired, she was a pretty girl. Many had been in love with her, but she thought highly of herself and had remained chaste. Nevertheless, since Heichū courted her single-heartedly, she gave herself to him. The next morning he did not even send the customary letter. By night he still had sent no word. She was awake and miserable all night, and she waited all the next day, yet he still did not so much as send her a letter. She waited in anticipation that night, and yet ... The next morning her servants were saying to each other, "After all this time she has given herself to another, and to a man who we have heard acts in a most irresponsible manner. Even if he cannot find time to come in person, he could at least send a letter! A miserable affair indeed!" Upon hearing her own inner thoughts spoken by others, she cried in misery and frustration. She waited again that night on the slim hope that he would come, but he did not. Nor did he send a letter the next day. In all, five or six days passed with no word from him. The woman did nothing but weep, and she ate not a thing. Her servants told her, "Now just do not think about it. This small matter cannot be the end of things for one of your station. Just do not let anyone know about it, and marry someone else."

She secluded herself without a word, and out of sight of her own servants she snipped off her very long hair and became a nun at her own hand. Her servants gathered around and cried, but they could do nothing about it. "I want to die, miserable person that I am, but I cannot die," she said. "At least I can do this and follow the religious life. Do not make such a loud commotion."

As to how this had all come about, Heichū had intended to send a messenger to her early in the morning after he left her that night, but his office chief had come by, with a sudden plan to go somewhere, and found him sleeping. He aroused him with a remark about sleeping so late and took him off for a long walk and would not let him return home as they drank and caroused. No sooner had he finally gotten home again than he was escorted to Ōi in the company of the Teiji Mikado. There he attended the Mikado a further two nights and became terribly intoxicated. When they headed back, late at night, he intended to go to the lady's place, but the direction was impeded by a star of ill omen, and the people with the Mikado all went off together in an entirely different direction.

He thought longingly of Musashi and how uneasy and suspicious she must be. "If only night would fall," he thought, as his intoxication faded, "I will go myself and explain the situation. What is more, I will send a letter too." At that moment someone came and knocked on his door.

"Who is it?" he inquired.

"One with a message for the Second Assistant."

Heichū peeked out and saw that it was a woman from Musashi's house. He invited her in and took the letter she handed him to read, whereupon he found that the very fragrant paper was wrapped around a little of Musashi's hair, done up in a ring. He read, with foreboding, what was written there:

ama no kafa	The River of Heaven [the Milky Way],
sora naru mono to	so I have heard, is in the sky.
kikisikado	But no, it turns out to be
waga me no mafe no	the tears before my own eyes.
namida narikeri	

He saw, in a play on words, that this must mean that she had become a nun, and his very eyes dimmed.

Frantically he questioned the messenger. When she answered, crying, she said, "She has already cut off her hair. The Ladies of her household have been crying and terribly upset these two days because of it. It is heartbreaking even to my lowly servant's mind. Such long hair it was . . ."

He was stunned. He could only wonder why such a flirtation should bring about so sorry a result. Tearfully he wrote an answer:

yo wo waburu	No matter how fast your tears of
namida nagarete	frustration flow, can they become
fayaku to mo	as the River of Heaven [Can anything
ama no kafa ni fa	be so bad that one should become
sa ya fa naru beki	a nun]?

"I am so taken aback that I am quite speechless. I shall go there myself, at once," he said. And he went forthwith.

Meanwhile, Musashi had secluded herself in the plastered storehouse. Heichū told the servants how things were, and of his obstacles, and there were no bounds to his crying.

"I only want to speak to you. At least say something," he told her, but she made not the slightest answer. It seemed to him that she must still think, not knowing what obstacles had beset him, that he was just speaking out of pity, and it was a most terrible experience for him.

(142) A sister of the late Royal Concubine, the one who was the eldest daughter, was very talented and her poetry excelled even that of her younger brothers and sisters including the Concubine herself. Her mother had died when she was young. Since she was placed in the care of a stepmother, there were times when things did not go in accord with her feelings. And she composed this poem:

arifatenu	If only I could wait out
inoti matu ma no	just the period of my
fodo bakari	remaining life

uki koto sigeku	without too much
nagekazu mo gana	melancholy and grief.

Another time she plucked a plum blossom and composed this:

kakaru ka no	If such fragrance as this
aki mo kafarazu	lasted unchanged into autumn,
nifofi seba	would one sigh that she
faru kofisi tefu	longed for the spring?
nagame semasi ya	

Since she was a very well-bred and delightful person there were a great many people courting her, but she did not respond to them. Her father and stepmother both told her that there was more to being a woman and that she should respond occasionally. Thus badgered, she sent this poem to one man:

omofedomo	I suppose people consider
kafi nakaru bemi	me cold, for even though I
sinobureba	love, I recognize that love as
turenaki to mo ya	hopeless and keep it to
fito no miru ramu	myself.

Her letter said only this, and nothing more.

What she meant was that, though her parents wanted to marry her to someone, she would never marry; she always said so, and precisely as she said, she passed away at twenty-nine, never having married.

(149) Once there were a man and a woman who lived in Kataragi District, Yamato Province. The woman's face and features were very fair. They had been in love and he had lived with her for years, when this woman became very poor. Because of that, the man, tormented and loving her boundlessly all the while, found a second wife elsewhere. The new wife was a rich woman. He did not love her especially, but when he went to see her she took great pains for him and kept his personal effects clean. He grew accustomed to that prosperous place, and when he would come back his first wife seemed very poor. And because she did not seem at all jealous even though he kept going to the other place, he found it very touching. The truth was that she kept her feelings of boundless jealousy and misery to herself.

Since she still said "Go" even on nights when he thought he would stay, he wondered in his heart if, instead of being jealous of his travels, she was seeing someone else in his absence—otherwise she should resent his going. Then he made a show of going out, but hid in the shrubbery in front of the house to see if a man would come. She came out on the veranda and remained there combing her hair under a very pleasant moon. Since she stayed up very late and lingered there very wistfully, it looked to him as if she were waiting for someone. Then she said to her servant, who was in front of her:

kaze fukeba	He must now be crossing
oki tu siranami	Tatsuta Mountain
tatutayama	all alone in the middle of the night.
yofa ni ya kimi ga	
fitori koyu ramu	

When she had composed this, the man realized that she had been thinking of him and he was sorrow-stricken. His other wife's house was on the road that goes over Tatsuta Mountain.

Then, as he continued to watch, the woman threw herself down, crying, and she filled a metal bowl with water and set it on her breast. "What on earth can she be doing?" the man wondered, still watching. Then the water began to steam and boil, and she poured it out. Again she filled the bowl. It was too sad to watch, and he ran out. "What feelings can make you do such a thing?" he asked, and sweeping her into his arms, he lay down with her. After that he stayed with her and did not go to the other woman any more.

Much time passed and then the man thought, "I have found that a woman can be feeling terrible things even though she wears an indifferent expression. I wonder how my other wife feels about my not going there anymore?" He went to the other woman's house. He had not gone there for so long that he was hesitant about going in. He peeked in and saw that although she had always looked her best for him, she was wearing clothing of very shabby appearance, she had a large comb holding the hair from her forehead in the manner of common folk, and she was dishing up her food with her own hand. He was shocked by this, and he came back never to go there again. This man was a scion of the royal family.

(157) A man and a woman lived in Shimotsuke Province. After living with her for years, the man established another wife and his feelings for the first one changed completely. He swept up all of the things that he had in her house and carried them to his new wife's place. Though she was miserable about it, the first wife let him have his way and just watched. He went away with everything,

leaving not so much as a speck of dust. The only thing he left was just a horse's drinking vessel. And the man even sent his retainer, a lad named Makaji, to get the vessel. The woman remarked to the lad that she would not see him there anymore either, but he stood there and said that he did not see why he could not call on her even if his master was no longer there. Then the woman said, "Would you give your master a message for me? He would never read a letter. Just tell him aloud." When the lad said that he certainly would, she said to tell him this:

fune mo inu	The vessel is going away.
makadi mo miezi	Nor will I see the scull ["scull"
kefu yori fa	is homophonous with the boy's name]
uki yo no naka wo	again. How will I traverse
ikade wataru ramu	the miserable world after today?
	["miserable world" can also be taken
	"world where I float" to carry
	on the boat and scull imagery.]

When the lad told the man, this man who had gone off with all those things carried back every single thing and stayed with the woman as before, never looking at another woman.

(168) During the reign of the Fukakusa Mikado, Captain Yoshimine was extremely influential. [. . .] At a time when he was considered a man of faculty by the world at large and boundlessly esteemed by the Mikado he served, this same Mikado passed away. On the night of the Royal Funeral, while everybody was in attendance, this Captain Yoshimine disappeared. His friends and wives wondered what had happened to him and searched everywhere for some time, but there was no sign of him. They thought that he might have become a Buddhist monk or he might have drowned himself, but if he had become a monk they should have had some word of it; therefore he must have drowned himself. The whole world felt sorrow at this thought, to say nothing of his wives and children. They performed purifications and ritual abstentions day and night and frantically offered devotions to the Buddhas and gods of the world, but nothing was heard of him. Yoshimine had three wives. To the two of whom he was only moderately fond he had said, "I do not think I care to go on living in the world." He gave not the slightest hint of such feelings to the wife he loved boundlessly and who had borne his children. He was afraid that if he told

her, he would not be able to carry out his plan in the face of her distress, so he vanished without even coming to see her. This wife thought that it had been terrible of him not to have told her how he felt, no matter what, and crying and fuming about it all the while, she went to Hatsuse Temple. This was at a time when the Captain happened to be at the Temple, for he had indeed become a monk and had traveled throughout the land practicing his religion with only a mino on his back. He overheard his wife tell the priest in charge of memorial services, ". . . and that is the last we heard of him. If he is still among the living, let us see each other once more. If he has killed himself, let me see, in reality or dream, how he is." She was offering all the Captain's clothing, even his formal attire, girdles and swords, in return for sutra chanting, and her speech gave way to anguished sobbing.

At first the Captain had been listening to discover who might have come to worship, but now sorrow overwhelmed him as she spoke of his affairs like this and gave away his clothing. "Might I run out to her?" he wondered a thousand times, but each time he thought better of it and stayed where he was, in tears all night long. He could still hear his wife and children speaking. His distress was profound. But he endured the night, crying until morning, and then he saw that the tears that had fallen on his mino and elsewhere were tears of blood. "So there really are such things, the 'tears of blood' from intense crying!" he said. He was to remark later that he had felt he just had to run out to them at that juncture.

Try as she would, the woman was unable to learn anything of her husband. Presently the period of mourning for the Mikado ended. A great crowd of people from the Palace had gone out to the river for the ablutions necessary when removing mourning clothes, when an odd-looking boy came up carrying a piece of oak with writing on it. Someone took it and read:

mina fito fa	I hear that everyone else
fana no koromo ni	has changed to flowery robes.
narinu nari	Oh, you moss [-colored monk's]
koke no tamoto yo	sleeves [still wet with tears],
kawaki dani seyo	dry up at least.

The handwriting was recognized as that of Captain Yoshimine. They wanted to question the boy who had brought the poem, but though they searched far and wide, he was nowhere to be found.

With this, people realized that the Captain must have become a monk. Nevertheless, no one had any idea where he was. The Consort heard that he was still alive, and she sent a Court valet to search for him in the many monasteries. Whenever the valet heard that the Captain was at a certain place and went there to see, the Captain had vanished again. The valet was unable to meet him. At long last the valet chanced upon the place where the Captain was hiding. Unable to remain hidden, he came out to see the valet. The valet told him that he had come as a messenger from the Consort and related her message: "Since the Mikado is gone and all that remains to me are those persons for whom he had affection, I am grieved that you have vanished and hidden yourself away from the world. Why is it that, even though you are engaging in religious practices in the wilderness, you give us no tidings? I hear that they are weeping and languishing at the place that was your home for lack of news from you. What kind of man are you to cause such anguish?" The monk, weeping, said, "I respectfully acknowledge the royal message. The Mikado's sacred presence was so much a part of my world that I felt I could no longer live in it after he had departed. I came away to the end of the earth, alone, and waited to die, but strangely enough I still live on. I am deeply grateful that the Consort deigned to inquire after me. And I have never for a moment forgotten my family. Please report that I said:

kagiri naki	Even though I am far from
kumowi no yoso ni	the Court, I still carry
wakaru to mo	everyone with me in my heart.
fito wo kokoro ni	
okurasamu ya fa	

The valet felt an unparalleled sadness on seeing the present condition of the priest. He had become but a shadow of his former self, and he was wearing only a mino. The valet remembered how impeccable his appearance had been when he was a Captain, and he could not restrain his tears. Yet sad though he was, he could not waste a moment if he was to get out of the mountain depths and back to Court, and he bade the priest a tearful farewell. When he got back he had it reported to the Consort how he had found the monk and what the monk had said. The Consort cried with much anguish, and so did those serving her weep fretfully and feel deeply touched. She tried to send him an answer together with messages from many others, but he was no longer where he had been.

Ono no Komachi, the famed beauty and poet, went to worship,

at the beginning of a certain year, at Kiyomizu. She was saying her prayers when she heard an unusually refined priest's voice reading sutras and dharanis. She was suspicious and, in a casual manner, sent someone to see. She was told that it was a monk wearing only a mino with a flint-box tied on at the waist. The more she listened, the more noble and well-favored the voice sounded, making her think, "This could never be a commoner; I wonder if it is the Captain monk?" To find out what he would reply she sent someone to tell him, "I am cold here at the temple. Please lend me something to wear":

ifa no ufe ni	It is very cold sleeping on
tabine wo sureba	the rocks away from home.
ito samusi	I hope that you will lend me
koke no koromo wo	a robe of moss.
ware ni kasanamu	

To this he replied:

yo wo somuku	Having turned my back on the
koke no koromo fa	world, I have but one robe
tada fitofe	of moss. I should be heartless
kasaneba turasi	not to lend it to you. Come then,
iza futari nemu	we shall sleep together.

At this she was all the more certain that it was the Captain, and she decided, since they had been on speaking terms, to go and talk with him. But when she went, he had vanished without a trace. She made search for him throughout the temple, but he had fled and vanished completely.

(173) Captain Yoshimine no Munesada was going somewhere when, because it began to rain heavily about the time he was passing Fifth Avenue, he took shelter in a dilapidated gateway and peered inside. There was a bark-thatched house five spans square with a godown attached, but there was no person in sight. He walked in and saw a plum tree in very delightful bloom near the steps; a warbler was singing there as well. Behind blinds where he would not have expected anyone to be, someone wearing a light violet robe over a dark red one, a person of good height, whose hair seemed as long as herself, said to herself:

yomogi ofite	The warbler sings
aretaru yado wo	that someone comes,
ugufisu no	though to a dilapidated lodge

fito ku to naku ya	overgrown with mugwort.
tare to ka matamu	But whom should I expect?

The Captain said in a pleasant tone:

kitaredomo	I was already here,
ifi si nareneba	but because I am not used
ugufisu no	to saying so, the warbler was
kimi ni tugeyo to	singing to teach me
wosifete zo naku	to tell you.

The woman was startled. She had thought no one was there, and feeling that she had let herself be seen at her worst, she fell silent. The man went up onto the veranda. "Why do you not speak?" he said. "It is raining altogether too hard, and I thought that until it ceased . . ." She replied, "It leaks considerably more in here than in the street, I fear." The time was about the tenth day of the first month. She thrust a cushion out through the blinds, and he pulled it to him and sat down. The borders of the blinds had been nibbled on by bats and were missing here and there. He looked in at the furnishings. The matting had been good in its day, but was now less than satisfactory.

It had begun to grow dark, and he slid silently inside and would not let the woman go into the back part of the house. The woman was vexed, but she had no way to restrain him, and what happened was inevitable. It rained all night long, and then the sky cleared a little early in the morning. When the woman tried to go into the back part of the house, he told her to stay just as she was and he would not let her go.

When the sun was high, the woman's parents, lacking the means to give their guest the Captain a proper feast, gave to the young valet he had kept with him rock salt to eat and sake to drink, and for the Captain they picked some of the herbs that were growing in the large yard and prepared them by steaming. They served them to him in a bowl, and for chopsticks they broke off blossom-covered branches of the plum tree. On the petals of the blossoms this was written in a very delightful feminine hand:

kimi ga tame	These are young herbs I picked
koromo no suso wo	for you, getting the hem of
nurasitutu	my garment wet as I went into
faru no no ni idete	the spring moors to pick them.
tumeru wakana zo	

The man felt very moved on reading this, and pulling the food to him, he ate. The woman was immoderately self-conscious and knelt with her face turned low. The Captain got up and sent his young valet running on an errand. The valet returned shortly with a wagon-load of various practical articles. Then, since someone had come to get him, the Captain said he would come again soon and he left.

After that he incessantly visited her in person. He had eaten a myriad kinds of food, but he thought that the food at Fifth Avenue was more wonderful and admirable than any.

Years later the Captain was bereft of the Lord whom he served, and not wanting to see the succeeding reign, he became a monk. He once sent his monk's stole to the woman of this story for washing, and with it this poem:

simo yuki no	It is the dark-eyed hempen
furuya no moto ni	stole in which I now sleep
fitorine no	alone, in another old house.
utubusizome no	
asa no kesa nari	

Tanikawa Shuntarō

FOUR POEMS

TRANSLATED BY HAROLD WRIGHT

INTRODUCTION

TANIKAWA SHUNTARŌ, the only son of a philosopher, was born December 15, 1931, in Tokyo.

At an early age Shuntarō displayed his intellectual prowess; in the second primary school in Tokyo, he was often at the head of the class, although he later admitted not having enjoyed school. At this time he began to spend summers in North Karuizawa near the famed volcano, Mt. Asama, a place celebrated by poets a generation before him.

In 1945, as the air raids on Tokyo increased, Shuntarō, aged fifteen, learned at first hand about the ravages of war as he bicycled around the ruins, in which charred bodies remained. He was evacuated to Kyoto with his mother in July of that year. The following year he returned to Tokyo, where he resumed his middle-school education.

At the age of eighteen, with the encouragement of friends, Shuntarō began to write poetry. Within a year his growing dislike for school became overt: his grades began to deteriorate, and he occasionally quarrelled with his teachers. Finally he changed schools and continued as a part-time student. Although he finished high school, he had no desire to attend the university.

With an introduction from Miyoshi Tatsuji in December, 1950, Shuntarō began publishing individual poems such as "Nero" in the magazine *Bungakkai* (Literary World). His first book of poetry appeared in 1952; the twenty-one-year-old poet entitled his work *Nijuoku Konen no Kodoku* (Twenty Billion Light Years of Loneliness). The next year *Rokujūni no Sonetto* (Sixty-Two Sonnets) was published, and he joined the magazine *Kai* (Oar).

In 1955 Shuntarō ended a year-old marriage and offered his readers a new volume of poetry, *Ai ni Tsuite* (Concerning Love). He also began to write radio plays. Expanding his perspective still further,

Shuntarō published in 1956 a collection of his own photographs and poems entitled *Ehon* (Picture Book).

Okubo Tomoko became Shuntarō's second wife in 1957. At this time he wrote a book of essays, *Ai no Panse* (Thoughts of Love). He built a home in Tokyo the following year.

Sekai E (To the World), a collection of essays concerning poetry, was added to Shuntarō's rapidly increasing repertoire in 1959. In 1960 he produced a book of poems entitled *Anata Ni* (To You) as well as a three-act comedy; and in this same year his son was born.

In 1961 Shuntarō's satirical poems on current subjects became a regular feature of the *Shukan Asahi* (The Asahi Weekly). *21*, a volume of verse, came out in this year as did a book of essays, *Adamu to Ibu no Taiwa* (A Dialogue between Adam and Eve).

In 1964 he published *Rakushu Kujuku* (Satirical Poems Ninety Nine) and participated in the filming of the Tokyo Olympics. In 1965 Shuntarō, who now had a second child—a two-year-old daughter—produced a book of children's poems, *Nihongo no Okeiko* (Japanese Lessons) and a children's story. Also *Tanikawa Shuntarō Shisho* (Selected Poems of Tanikawa Shuntarō) was published.

When he visted Western Europe and the United States on a Japan Society grant in 1966, Shuntarō found that Americans assumed automatically that a Japanese poet wrote *haiku*. At this time he began plans for a translation of modern Japanese poetry into English.

Shuntarō was no less prolific a writer after his return to Japan. In 1967 he published a collection of short stories and wrote a film script, *Kyo* (Kyoto).

In January of the following year *Ai no Shishu* (Collection of Love Poems) appeared. The *Tanikawa Shuntarō Shishu* (Poems of Tanikawa Shuntarō) became available in August, and a smaller collection of selected poems appeared in December. A collection of poems and photographs, *Tabi* (Journey), came out in November, 1968.

Tanikawa Shuntarō represented Japan in the International Poetry Festival that was held at the Library of Congress in Washington, D.C., on April 13, 14, 15, 1970. The poems that follow are selected from those that he and I read there.

TANIKAWA SHUNTARŌ / FOUR POEMS

SADNESS II

Sadness
A half-peeled apple
Not a metaphor
Not a poem
Merely there
A half-peeled apple
Sadness
Merely there
Yesterday's evening paper
Merely there
Merely there
A warm breast
Merely there
Nightfall
Sadness
Apart from words
Apart from the heart
Merely there
The things of today.

REQUEST

Turn inside out   turn me
Plow the fields inside me
Dry up the wells inside me
Turn inside out   turn me
Wash out my insides
And maybe you'll find a splendid pearl
Turn inside out   turn me
Is the inside of me the sea?
Is it the night
Is it a distant road
Is it a polyethylene bag
Turn inside out   turn me

What is growing inside of me
A field of overripe cactus plants?
A premature offspring of a unicorn?
A buckeye tree that failed to become a violin?
Turn inside out   turn me
Make the wind blow through me
Let my dreams catch cold
Turn inside out   turn me
Let my concepts weather away.

Turn inside out
Turn inside out please   turn me
Please shelter my skin
My forehead is frostbitten
My eyes are red with bashfulness
My lips are weary of kisses
Turn inside out
Turn inside out please   turn me
Let my insides worship the sun
Spread my stomach and pancreas over the grass
Evaporate the reddened darkness!
Stuff the blue sky into my lungs!
With my spermaduct all entangled
Have me trampled by black stud horses
Please have my heart and brain,
        using chopsticks of plainwood,
Be eaten by the one I love

Turn inside out
Turn inside out please   turn me
Let all the words within me
Be chatted completely away   and quickly
Let the singing quartet of instruments
Be resounded completely away
Let the aged birds within me
be flown completely away
Let the love within me
Be lost in an evil gambling den.

Turn inside out, please turn, inside out, turn me
I give away the fake pearl inside me

So turn inside out, please turn, inside out, turn me
Silence alone speaks softly within me
Let me depart
Outside of myself
To that shade of trees
Over that woman
Into that sand.

LOVE
for Paul Klee

Forever
for so long, forever
bound for so far
for so long, for so far, joined together
for sake of the weak
for sake of those in love but separate
or those who live alone
forever
for so long, forever, we need unending song
so heaven and earth will not quarrel
so the separate will be joined again
for the return of a single heart to the people's heart
and trenches to ancient villages
and the sky to innocent birds
and fairy tales to little children
and honey to the diligent bee
and the world to the things without names
for so far
for so long, for so far, joined together
as if about to end itself completely
as if about to perfect itself completely
forever like the blueprint of god
for so long, forever, approaching perfection
so all can be joined together
so all separate things will cease to be
so all can continue to live under one name:
the tree and the woodcutter

the young girl and blood
the window and love
the song and another song
so that quarreling is over
to end the useless things for sake of life
in such plentifulness
for so long, forever, that image spreads
as if to have the world become the imitator,
the image that beckons with a gentle glance.

SONNET 45

When the wind is strong
The earth resembles someone's kite;
Even during the full noon hours
People feel already the night is there.

The wind is without words,
It merely whirls around and frets.
I think of wind on another star
Wondering if they can form a friendship.

On earth there is nighttime and the day
What do other stars do during these times?
How can they bear to spread in silence?

By day the blue sky is telling lies
While night mutters the truth, we sleep
And when morning comes we say we've dreamed.

Kusano Shimpei

THREE POEMS WITH SOUNDS &
REPORT OF A CERTAIN DEATH

TRANSLATED BY KAMAIKE SUSUMA & CID CORMAN

KUSANO SHIMPEI (1903———) has written numerous volumes of poetry as well as essays, novels, stories, and criticism; he has edited the works of other poets, taught, translated, and lectured; he has run bars and eating stands and a large number of poetry mags; he has traveled widely and lived for two long periods in China (1921–25, 1940–46); he is the central spirit of the Rekitei poetry group and a member of the Japanese PEN club executive committee.

POEMS BY KUSANO SHIMPEI

3 POEMS WITH SOUNDS

I: BLUE JINTA*

a rugged peaked mountain of rock. in almost
equilateral triangle eastward towers. at its
base extends a limitless waste known as the
Place of Ashes. in the South and North Vietnam
War there three hundred years ago but. also
because of war upon war thereafter the number of
human beings was appreciably diminished. there
were lots of mixed marriages. pure blacks or
pure Japanese rarely found.

now. in the Place of Ashes a spiral glass tower
stands. pennants with "midsummer craziness"
flutter atop. eighteen parcels of felt. rigged
in a crescent but. one for the jinta shack. the
other seventeen resting places for frogs.

(originally frogs preferred temperate zones. tropical
zones. subtropical zones and moisture but. since
the 1900s those like the spade-foot toad have burrowed
into the desert country around Arizona.) wine-colored
twilight came on. the spiral glass tower was lit by
arterial red and blue neon and then the "funny circus"
of illuminated news flew through the air the frogs
swarmed from their seventeen resting places.

•

the jinta made up of clarinet cornet bass-drum and
　tambourine blares away &.
(the commonest kind without a big fat boss or a
　madman or a gangling slave.)
the jinta blares away &.
a frog a deadringer for Marilyn Monroe begins to
　sing her come-on.

* a small raggle-tail music troupe and their makeshift music

　　　　the new earth steaming.
　　　　every day every night hot springs.
　　　　lepidodendra for fans.
　　　　fanning hot flesh.

　　　　till earth feels cool.
　　　　scorpions wanting to bay at the moon.
　　　　black mist through city flowing.
　　　　lung-cancer chuckling.

(old! old!)
(marvellous! queen bee.)
this is really 20th century stuff.

suddenly Gambi leaps 15 yards. coming
down with a twirl like an ice-skater.
– dont need a ladder.
– nor a big cellophane net.
nor a rope nor frankly even a trapeze to sit on
but.
suddenly now a swing for six.
the jinta blaring away &.
just six jostling each other.
floating swinging seaweed cookies.
　　　　yun yun yun yuyuyun
　　　　yun yun yuyuyun
in the air song beginning to flow.

　　　　the Ashura heaven immense.
　　　　look. immense.
　　　　with all that moisture.
　　　　praise the great air!
　　　　look!

everywhere litmus blue &.
the spiral glass neon in a flash lights more &.
over the top of the peaked mountain a full moon.
(much more pockmarked than in 20th century nights.)
all over the wasteland so much diamond dust.
the jinta blaring away &.
in the midst of the Place of Ashes is Himulali tho.

in the blazing heart.
oenothera makiana.
the moon-colored flower.

the mirage lake ripples.
the sad stretch of it.
in your heart.

my moon-colored.
flower float.

(eh—. *sembei** and caramels.)

– somebody seems to be crazy somewhere.
lemonade and *sembei* vendors, etc., there arent any.
(ok. I'll give it the old traditional try.)

In the heavenly
brilliance in the breath of
a perfect spring day
the quiet heart is undone
with cherry blossoms falling.

(dont mock. the feeling's no good.)
(classic. great.)
(mockery's a vice. vice.)

the jinta blaring away &.
in the great space with a hop skip and a jump.
one after another bewilderingly.
the one leaping last a limping beauty.

(hey Lilimu. your asshole's showing.)
(wa! ha! ha!)
(wa! ha! ha!)
(wa! ha! ha!)

the jinta blaring away &.
the chorines beginning.

* Japanese rice biscuits

   like man with a belly-button.
   like man growing hair.
   the chorus making a ring in the Place of Ashes.
   viscera wiggling transparently.
      ahahahahahah.
      blare away cornet bass-drum.
      now all of you.
      like man have fallen.
      rararan rararan rararararan
      rararan rararan rararararan
   (hey! cut it out. stop.)
   a deep voice booms out.
   the "honest march" of electric news flowing in the air.

      our brains are little but.
      our hearts big (we've got plenty of nerve).
      on this side and the other of the earth.
      we're smiling.
         marchons marchons marchons
      we've got no weapons but.
      our lives rise and fall.
      in the hot wastes and gasp but.
         marchons marchons marchons
      beget. flourish. go on. go on.
   in scrimmages (diamond dust fragmentation)
   thousands of frogs surge forth.
   the jinta shrieks and reaches climax.
   in the air.
   snake fireworks begin to run.
   ten thousand firework snakes.
   shooshoopon shooshooshoosh confusion.
   from the top of the peaked mountain.
   with booo-whaam big cascading fireworks.
   casting out nets.

   shrieking jinta.
   smoking full moon.
   on earth big waves of frogs of waves.

II. THE BROKEN ORGAN

I've loved the intense.
winter.
summer.
the intense.
the seasons these two.

(the cannonade clouds seen supine in a boat of
        fixed seats.)
(the slashing hail that stung and stuck to my
        cheeks.)

now well along in life.
birds of prey behind.
to be drowned in fish.
pick wild rocambole and replant them in the fields.
dote on October's small seamy eggplants.

declining autumn's.
gold green bronze powdery.
sunlight seething in underbrush.
jays crying.

63 years already.

do
re
mi
fa
sol
la
ti
do

the high *do*. broken.

from the broken nose a faint/soft voice's.
plaintiveness.

(vomit.)

the ultimate climax became a far dream.

half-dead.

faint
off
faint
off

in the body were raging nebulae once.

now.

in my twilight a last cloud flag hanging.

III: HACHIJO* RHAPSODY

    dadadan dadadan dadadan dadadan
nightwind-licked Kurashio crawling up field &.
three bonfires blazing.
cra-ra-rackling.
flames swinging.
    dan dan dan dan
boys leopard-skins round their waists.
drumsticks carving the wind &.
    dan dan dadadan
(dancing dance barebreasted crescent moon upon you.)
big August festival of life.
dance. drink. devour. drink. devour. dance.
a giant tossing dried mackerel into his gaping gullet.
(eating *ta-go-be*† too. taro. and so much bamboo-shoot
    potato)
from a *jomon*‡ cup demon-killing liquor.
big woman guzzling loads of rice brandy.
(hot mist burning belly) young female deer. snivelling imps.
let yourself go old women! topaz women. dance dance.

---

* Hachijo is an island off Tokyo, famed as a place of exile, now a summer resort.
† all the foods are country vegetable delicacies
‡ old rope-pattern pottery

    wheel of the sun ahdoro ahdoro ahdoro.
    wheel of the moon ginga ginga ginga.
    praised be heaven and earth!
    O Gods. sing.

lice in the wild hair clinging to the shaking crawling
    into pores &.
crescent jade necklace swinging at breasts yun yun pulling
    torn off.

    dan dan dan dan dan dan dan kakaka dan
    kakaka dan kakakakah dan kakakat dan dan kat
    dan ka dan dan dan dan dan dan dan dan kakakat

    oh. praise fire.
    praise wind.
    praise water.
    praise earth.
    praise sea turtle and bracken.
    praise the life in all that lives.
    praise cunnus and penis.
    praise the sky and heaven and star.

    dan dan dadadan

Brahms' satellite rising.
from the dark dead end of heaven's line.
along the shores of the Milky Way.
through the center of the Swan's belly and lost in
    the depths of heaven.
oh. the long past and the long future mingle and make
    what is new strong. da da da.
yesterday and today lolling and languishing make what
is new weak. da da da.

bonfires blazing sound.

(pasania wood. camphorwood burn anything.)
    dan dan dan dan
Hachijo night unadvancing.

satellite of Brahms!
friend of the *Kojiki!**
    dadadan dadadan dadadan dadadan

REPORT OF A CERTAIN DEATH

Leah.
Leah's dead.

holding Leah in my right hand. pouring tablesalt into her
open mouth. put in a basin on the study floor. for all
the aquarium pump's bubble bubble air at her face Leah's
mouth opening opening. her gills already motionless.

Leah.
Leah's now slippery cold solid body. resting in my
two hands. all shining opaline &.
pale cerulean swimming in the opaline &.
near the dorsal fin blueblack spots like moles and
    a cometlike straight line.
& her eyes.
curious perfect black circles.
curdled blue *sumi*-drops—what pupils.

Where in Leah is death?
Where is death kept?
is there nowhere together life and death?
has death gone somewhere else through Leah?
the death gone through into my palms electrical &.
into my heart's old cavern crept?

Leah whose death's begun to live.
Leah done with death.

sleet slicked.
pulling Leah out of the pool with a big spoon-net.
her body already stiffly arched.
usually lying on back or side but.

* the old legendry

Leah upright listing at about 80°.
(strong heart)
standing dead.

Leah.
one day you were standing on the lawn by the fan ledge.
and I on this side of the pool.
(there. that one's Leah. heading this way. look look.)
pointing at one of them swimming in a group I.
(some resemblance eh?)
said to you.
huhuhu.
as if embarrassed you half-laughed but.
seemed to see your name in it.

here's Leah now.
myself back at the basin.
not to bring it back to life.
but to see it wrapped in her native water for
a while before being wrapped soon in soil.

near the stove the glass door clouds from within.
reflecting in its mottled openings. snow-mingled.
Akitsu* sleet.

(26 Dec. 1967)

* the suburb—rather rural—of Tokyo in which the poet lives.

THE MANUHARI JĀTAKA-TALE

TRANSLATED BY JOHN R. KRUEGER

INTRODUCTION

THE MANUHARI tale, never before translated, presents an interesting example of the "birth-story" (Sanskrit, *jātaka*) as developed among the Oirats or Western Mongols. The Oirat nation occupied Western Mongolia (Dzungaria) in the centuries after the fall of Chinggis (Genghis) Khan, and around 1630 a sizable faction resettled on the lower reaches of the Volga and Don rivers. These, known as Kalmyks, continue to live in the present region as an autonomous Soviet republic, although in 1771 large numbers returned to Mongolia and accepted Manchu-Chinese rule. However, both groups share the same language and literature.

Oirat-Mongolian literature began in 1648, when the lama-monk, Zaya Pandita, created for his people a divergent and more precise form of the old vertical Mongolian script, and began a program of translation and publication in it. It was actively used until the early years of this century, when increasing Russification and general change in society brought about its decline. In Kalmyk Republic of the Soviet Union, a Cyrillic alphabet based on Russian is now in use, and in Mongolia (the present-day Mongolian People's Republic) too, the old standard script has been supplanted by a Cyrillic version. Probably not more than 200 different literary and religious works in Oirat script survive. Copies of many are in Mongolian manuscript collections in Germany and other countries, but I do not know of any in the United States, except for photocopies from European holdings in my own possession. Very little of Oirat-Mongolian literature has been translated for English or Western readers, and translation of this tale, a representative literary work of the culture, will serve to introduce the English-speaking reader to this literary tradition.

The Mongols follow Buddhism in its Lamaistic form as developed in Tibet. A large part of their literature is an outgrowth of this religion and is often didactic, seeking to impart to society the values of a culture which considers seeking rebirth to a higher plane to be a main goal of existence. A story of the Buddha in one of his previous births, like the Manuhari tale, serves to draw attention to the practice of basic Buddhist virtues. The Mongol thus joins with other Buddhists of China, Tibet, and South East Asia through mutual sharing of a vast Buddhistic popular nondogmatic literature.

The form and content of a birth-story is generally fixed along the following lines. Lord Buddha is dwelling in his pleasure-park when, one day, some of his disciples engage him in conversation, and ask a question on morals or conduct. By way of illustration, the Buddha relates a story, often about a king or wealthy householder who was faced with a problem or who took an action along the lines of the original question. When the tale is concluded and the right moral action has been illustrated, we learn that the identities of the characters in the story correspond to the Buddha and his close associates, relatives, or even enemies in a prior rebirth, or cycle of reincarnation: "I was that king, and you, Ananda, were my...."

A considerable body of such tales has made its way into Mongolian, as the story-cycles, known generally by their Sanskrit names, the *Pancatantra* or "Five Fable Books," and the *Vetalapancavimsati*, "Twenty-five Goblin Stories," the latter also found in an Oirat recension. The Manuhari tale is a version of one called the *Sudhana-avadana*.*

The text itself is found in an original manuscript of 23 folios, acquired by Baron Asch and presented to the University Library at Göttingen (West Germany) in 1807.† It is a beautifully executed

---

* For parallels in Indian languages, the interested reader may see volume 29 (1966) of the *Bulletin of the School of Oriental and African Studies* (London), for the article by H. W. Bailey, "The Sudhana Poem of rddhiprabhava" (pp. 506–532), and of Padmanabh S. Jaini, "The Story of Sudhana and Manohara..." (pp. 533–558).

† A copy closely agreeing with this one is found in Dresden (East Germany), in the Saxony State Library. The Marburg (West Germany) Library has a hand-written copy made by B. Julg from the Dresden manuscript, and another copy made from this manuscript by Berthold Laufer (September, 1900) was discovered by me in September, 1965, among Laufer's belongings in the Field Museum of Natural History, Chicago (see p. 177 of my "Catalogue of the Laufer Mongolian Collections in Chicago," in the *Journal of the American Oriental Society*, vol. 86, 1966).

specimen of Oirat calligraphy, and an illustration of one folio is reproduced herewith. The translation has been made from the Laufer copy, with reference to the Göttingen manuscript. The text is straightforward and uncomplicated, and there seemed to be no need to make a detailed edition with transcription, variants and explanations. There remain only two or three unclear words, and one somewhat obscure sentence, by which I have set question marks.

The Manuhari tale is noteworthy both for its literary merit and as an important example of Western Mongolian popular Buddhistic literature and can be appreciated by a wide audience of readers.

This type of story, though widespread and known to many levels of society, is not a native composition, and bears little relation to the genuine Mongolian folk compositions, like the typical heroic epics, In like manner, we cannot count Grimm's tales, Aesop's fables or even the Biblical parables as part of English or American literature, though they are also widely known in these countries.

To avoid the use of many technical and foreign terms that will disrupt the reader's pleasure, but at the same time to maintain the usefulness of the translation for the specialist, I use the following technique in translation. The foreign word is combined and hyphenated with its rough English equivalent. In this way the specialist will know what technical term is used, and the general reader can use the more common word. One such term is *bodhi*-sanctity, where *bodhi* is a Sanskrit term denoting a kind of religious enlightenment requiring a long explanation. Words in brackets indicate explanatory additions; words in parentheses give foreign words or their equivalents, or aid in better phrasing in English.

The reader may also note a peculiarity of Mongolian reflected in the translation: the narrative annoyingly shifts back and forth between two speakers, referring to both as "he." To avoid the constant addition of identification, I generally use the pronoun as it is always evident from the action who the speaker(s) must be.

Two more features of the original are perforce reflected in the translation. One is the practice of using a verb of statement or speech both before and after a quotation. The other is the fact that transition between events is sometimes abrupt or sharp, at least for a Western reader, because the event or intermediate step thus omitted is familiar to or subconsciously assumed by the native reader.

Last, the reader may feel, in some of the poetical sections of the final pages, that sometimes the phrases and sentences do not quite seem to make sense. The reason for this is that the quatrains are alliterative in the original, and the poet sometimes chose the imagery of key phrases more for their sound-value than their sense-value. This is what produces a certain disjointed air, in strictly logical terms.

THE MANUHARI JĀTAKA-TALE / HEREIN DWELLS THE TALE OF THE GODDESS MANUHARI WHO CLEANSES GRAVE SIN

I bow to the Lama and the Three Jewels.

The Saints among those who are reborn and who have found unthinkable and inexhaustible strength, having demonstrated the merit of striving well and their own strength, have led all sentients to an incomparable *bodhi*-sanctity, according to a plan, and are extremely wondrous to those of the world.

At a time early and long past, in the land of India, there were two (states), *Tabun Togolder* (Five Perfections) of the North and *Tabun Togolder* of the South. The one called *Tabun Togos* of the North became prosperous: field crops were plentiful; rain fell from time to time; there were no enemies on yonder side; disease and epidemic were nonexistent; and all the people gathered there. The others in that land, at a lake called *Ling-xotu,* were a Naga-king called *Eldeb Zuil Torolkitu* (having various kinds of creatures) and a very remarkable king, Nomci (Learned).

In the land of *Tabun Togolder* of the South, in contrast to this, field crops did not come up, they fought one another, and it was not very peaceful. Once the fifth king of Togos of the South thought to himself, "What is the reason for the king of the North being prosperous? What is the reason this land of mine has become disquieted?" he thought to himself. As he did not know, he beat the state drums in the palace, sent up a pennant, blew a horn, assembled all his own people, and said as follows in verse:

> Hear ye, my people assembled here. I am asking of you now
> A plan to make this southern land happy.
> If there be one who knows, let him speak.
> Is this not our constant idea?

> The northern land is prosperous;
> Crops always grow and rain falls;
> Man and beast are ever devoid of ills;
> Many people have gathered and are very happy.

> If you assembled here now know
> The differences between these two,
> Tell me without fail!
> Let me devise a plan to be happier than that land.

Thus he declaimed.

From amidst those assembled an old man supported by a cane arose and came, made obeisance to the king, and reported as follows:

> Oh great king, hear!
> As regards the tranquil land of the north,
> The incomparable king defends a regime of religion, and
> People whosoever heed the king's command.

> Furthermore, there is the lake called Ling-xotu there;
> It is evident there is a rich Naga-king within this lake;
> Specifically, the people of this land
> Are happy for precisely this reason.

"As for the reason for the unhappiness of those in the South, you, Oh King, do not act in accordance with doctrine; your tributaries do not heed your commands. Because there is no such Naga-king here, our misery has thus arisen," he reported.

The king said, "Is there a means to bring that rich Naga-king to this land?" The old man said, "There are indeed spellcasters who know the way to bring him."

Assembling all the spellcasters, however many, the king said, "Oh spellcasters grounded in Vairocana, do ye spellcasters bring here by the might of upadesa-sorcery the rich Naga-king of the north! If you are not able to bring him, I shall punish you," he said.

From amongst the spellcasters a yellow-bearded spellcaster said, "We local spellcasters cannot bring him. There is a snowy mountain, like unto a helmet, at the source of a river, and before it is a cliff similar to palms pressed together. In a grotto of that cliff dwells the king of the spellcasters, who has practiced spells for many years, and who bites serpents with his mouth. If you go and summon that spellcaster, he surely will be able to bring the Naga-king," he said.

When the king dispatched spellcasters to invite the king of the spellcasters, the spellcasters arrived there, and when they had explained the whys and wherefores of bringing the Naga-king, the grand spellcaster came to the king's palace.

The king spoke as follows to the spellcaster. "Do you know a means to bring the Naga-king of the north here?" he said. The spellcaster advised, "I can indeed do so. The upadesa-sorcery to summon him will demand 108 drugs, 108 poisons, one elephant-load of five-colored thread, and eight iron pickets the size of a standing man, and requires the skull of a man who died from swelling sickness, and building a lake in this land equal in size to Ling-xotu Lake and surrounded by trees. It will be necessary for all us spellcasters to execute spells intermittently," he reported.

Then the king had everything performed in accordance with what the spellcaster had said, and when the spellcasters were executing spells, the rich Naga-king of the north learned of it by prescience and wisdom, and thought to himself as follows. "On the night of the fifteenth of the month, I shall leave this my own happy land, and go to the suffering land of the south," he thought, and his mind was ill at ease.

First transforming himself into the shape of an eight-year-old boy, he came out at the edge of his own lake. Perceiving a huntsman at the edge of the lake, he said, "What is the name of this land? What is this land called? Are the people of this land happy or miserable? What is your name?", he inquired. The man said, "This land is the happy country Togos of the North. The beings of this land are very happy. I am a man who catches and eats fish from this lake," he said.

Then the Naga-king said, "What is the reason this land has been happy?" The hunter said, "The lord of this land is King Nomci. The king defends the realm by doctrine, and furthermore, there is a rich Naga-king within this Ling-xotu Lake. By virtue of these two reasons, the entire people is happy," he said. The Naga-king said, "In that case, when on the night of the fifteenth of this month, spellcasters who have woven spells come and take this your rich Naga-king to the south, will the people of the north protect him?" he inquired. The hunter said, "If spellcasters come and take this our rich Naga-king to the southern land, why won't everyone protect him?"

Thinking to himself, he said, "Since this hunter is a very sinful man, he surely will be able to slay the spellcasters when they come." [Then he said,] "I am he, your rich Naga-king. On the night of the fifteenth of this month, a spellcaster will come, confining every direction of the lake with eight iron pickets and netting it with five-colored thread, and will put 108 poisons in the attached skull of a man who died from swelling sickness. When he casts it into the lake, I shall be unable to endure the pestilence and will come out above the lake. At that time, you seize the spellcaster fearlessly by the hair and tell him as follows. 'You evil spellcaster, why are you defiling this our Lake Ling-xotu? If you will restore this lake to its original state, do so; if not, I shall slay you.' When you say this, the spellcaster will be afraid, and will weave a tranquil spell. At that time when he casts his 108 drugs into the lake, my illness will disappear. Just then you kill the spellcaster. Whatever *siddhi*-power you need, I shall bestow. You will make this land very happy," he said. The hunter promised [to do as he was told].

Then the grand spellcaster of the south, executing all his great needs, put five-colored thread on an elephant, loaded the iron pickets, the drugs, poisons and so on, took the upadesa-sorcery, and together with all his colleagues, went to bring back the Naga-king on the night of the fifteenth.

The grand spellcaster thought to himself, "Now these spellcasters have observed my entire sorcery. If they witness this sorcery now, my name will later not come to the fore," he thought, and said to his colleagues as follows. "You do not need to go there; return each to your home," he said. When he had them return, he proceeded alone.

Then the spellcaster came to the edge of the lake, and impaling the iron pickets at the four directions and the four intervals between, he spread out netting of five-colored thread. Placing 108 poisons in the attached skull of a man who died from swelling sickness, he blew and invoked a fierce spell, and cast it into the lake. Lake Ling-xotu seethed, and the rich Naga-king Eldeb Torolkitu was unable to endure the pestilence and came out above the lake.

The hunter, who was lurking about just then, suddenly appeared and seized the spellcaster by the hair, saying as follows. "Why are you tormenting our rich Naga-king? If you will leave this Naga-king in his previous state, do so; if not, I shall surely slay you," he said. The spellcaster was afraid, and said as follows. "Don't kill me. As for what way the lake and Naga-king were, I shall leave them like that," he said. He blew and invoked a tranquil spell on the 108 drugs, and when he cast them into the lake, the Naga-king's illness was cured. After he had cast them into the lake, the hunter killed the spellcaster, and using his bones as a pillow, he spent the night beside the lake.

In the morning when the sun rose, the Naga-king came and said to the hunter, "You have helped me. Now come to my palace." The hunter said, "I am unable to go into water." The Naga-king said as follows, "Let me take you by means of *rddhi*-magic," and taking him on his back, the Naga-king took him to his palace, seated the hunter on the jeweled throne, regaled him with all kinds of different foods, and said as follows.

> You saved my life from a clearly fearful enemy,
> Possessing secret and evident *rddhi*-magic;

Therefore, whatever awards you find suitable,
I shall repay your deed of merit openly.

When he presented him various kinds of jewels, that hunter was very happy and thought to himself, "Although I was formerly of lowly rebirth, and whereas I used to eat just game and fish, today the Naga-king has seated me on the jeweled throne within his palace and bestowed on me ever so many kinds of jewels. By the might of these jewels, I shall indeed be able to gratify the sentients of the Jambud-vipa-world. Is this a dream, or is it true? If this is a dream, don't let me wake up!" he thought to himself. Then the hunter said, "Oh thou Naga-king, you have repaid my good deed. Now send me to land," he said, and the Naga-king sent the hunter to land in a twinkling.

The hunter took the jewels and showed them to an old man and woman who lived in his own country. "Are these jewels which I found good or bad jewels? Look at them, you two," he said. They said as follows, "We two do not know about good and bad jewels. At the time when we were infants, at the source of a river, there was an old *rsi*-sage dwelling in *dhyana*-meditation. If he is still there now, he will know a great deal about good and bad jewels."

The hunter proceeded to go to that rsi-sage. In the grotto of the cliff called Guuri, which is at the source of a river, he found the sage, bowed and received his blessing, and when he had him investigate whether the jewels were good or bad, the sage spoke as follows. "These jewels are three-sided and five-sided, and there are many good lapis lazuli. Whence came so many jewels to you?" he said, and the hunter related his story in detail. "The Naga-king was extremely gracious to you," he declaimed.

The hunter said, "Oh most remarkable sage! An old man and woman at the foot and mouth of this river said to me that when they both were infants, you were an old man. Now, you have not grown extremely aged. By virtue of what has such occurred?" he asked. The sage declaimed, "In a land two or three leagues beyond here, there is a lake where the Esrua(Brahma)-gods gather and wash. There comes a girl seven times as fine as a human girl to wash her body. After that comes a girl seven times as fine as the Naga-maiden to wash. After that comes a girl seven times as fine as the heavenly maiden to wash her body. After that comes a girl seven times as fine as the Gandharva girl to wash. And after that comes the daughter of the Kinnara king, he of the horse's head (Hayagriva), who is far better than all of them.

"Her name is Manuhari. When you behold her, she is insatiably beautiful. Her body is adorned with various sorts of jewels. Every single strand of her hair is decorated each one with a jewel; and each one of the adorning jewels is impossible to be compared at all with the entire goods of the Jambudvipa-world. Such girls as this come to wash on an auspicious day of every month.

"At the time when these girls sing and dance the dance of the gods, the dance of the Nagas, the dance of the Gandharvas and the dance of the Kinnara, and when their music resounds to the waters flowing in that land, those waters flow softly and silently. The plants and trees, wafting in the wind, silently bend their tips to hear the girls' songs. The birds which are there, and tigers, leopards, bears, monkeys, *simin* [?] animals, and *pisaca*-vampires, *raksa*-demons, malevolent demons, *pretas* and others, all of them observe these girls' dances, listen to the music, and no harm befalls [anyone].

"Thus, when I drink the water of that lake, and wash my body, I do not seek food for seven sun-rounds because I am cleansed of all my faults and evils. The blessing of this water is why my life and age have become long," he declaimed. The hunter stated, "Oh grand sage, if it were possible to see this great sight, what a fine thing that would surely be," he said respectfully. The sage declaimed, "Tomorrow is the auspicious day. If I am not there, it will be impossible to see them. If you wish to observe, follow behind me tomorrow and watch," he said.

On the morrow the sage let the hunter follow him, and they concealed themselves in the spaces between the trees at the edge of the lake where the Esrua-gods gathered. While they were there, in accord with the sage's previous statement, before long there came through the sky one by one in turn a human maiden, a Naga-maiden, a Gandharva-maiden, and a very beautiful girl, seven times far more lovely than these, and they washed. After this, when the Kinnara king's daughter came, they danced the dance of the gods, the Naga dance, and the dances of Gandharvas, men, the big-bellied one and the jug-bellied one, and others. As for the place where they disported, an incomparably fine exhibition, like the opening of the monastery gates, was seen.

Then, after these maidens had gone back, the sage and the hunter returned to the grotto of the cliff. On the morning following this, the hunter stated, "Oh great sage, yesterday I saw a remarkable sight. How lovely were the beautiful girls and songs! Is there a way to catch one of them?" he asked. The sage declaimed, "There is a means to catch her. If you can get an efficacious jewel-sling, it will be possible to catch her," he said.

The hunter thought to himself as follows. "The Naga-king surely must have an efficacious jewel-sling. Let me seek and get it," he said. That night he found no repose. Early the next day he took his previous jewels and went to the edge of the lake. "Oh Naga-king!" he cried. The Naga-king made no sound. The hunter said, "If I go to the land of Tabun Togosuqsen of the south, there surely must be some one (there) like that former spellcaster." When he threatened thus, although the Naga-king knew by his prescient wisdom that there was no such great and powerful spellcaster, he said to himself, "This man was a person very helpful to me; if it be that there is something that he needs, I shall give it to him."

When the Naga-king came, the hunter said, "These jewels which you formerly gave me are not able to repay my good deed. If you will truly repay me, give me the efficacious jewel-sling," he said. The Naga-king said, "As for this efficacious jewel-sling, because of the danger of the King Garuda to us Nagas, this efficacious jewel-sling is our talisman. If we are without it, there is danger from the King Garuda." When he offered him two additional jewels, the hunter did not accept. "If you are going to give something, give the efficacious sling," he said and beseeched repeatedly.

The Naga-king brought the efficacious jewel-sling, placed it in the hunter's hands, and said as follows:

> The reason that this country is tranquil and happy
> Is the might of me, the supreme Naga-king.
> When a spellcaster was leading me helpless
> From here to the land of the south,
>
> When I was being taken to an unknown land,
> You had pity on me and saved me;
> I shall never be forgetful of your kind deed;
> Today I bestowed still more, the efficacious sling.

The hunter was very happy and spoke his reply:

> Knowing it has brought benefit is very remarkable;
> A Naga-king just like you is rare in the world;
> If much benefit has been brought, it is also rare like you;
> Giving the efficacious sling to me was very fine.

Bringing the efficacious sling, he spoke to the sage:

> Oh great sage who has pacified his senses!
> Oh you topmost adornment of sages without error!
> I have found the efficacious sling, difficult to find in this world.
> Now let us proceed to the lake where Esruas assemble.

The two of them on the next auspicious day took the efficacious sling and went to the edge of the lake. As they sat concealed among trees, there came a girl seven times more beautiful than a human girl, adorned with many ornaments and silkstuffs. When she was washing, the hunter said, "Let me seize her," but the sage restrained him and did not let him seize her. Then, when there came a girl far more beautiful than the Naga girl, the heavenly girl, and the Gandharva girl, he asked, "Shall I catch her?" and again the sage restrained and stopped him.

Soon after this came the daughter of the Kinnara king, surrounded by five hundred maidens, replete with parasols, banners [lit. 'victorious symbols'], guidons, lute and flute music, and so forth, ringing and tinkling, and adorned with various kinds of jewels. As they watched them dance the dance of the gods, the dance of the Nagas, the dance of the Gandharvas, etc., they danced insatiably, voicing fine and lovely melodies, and a beautiful, remarkable exhibition, like the opening of the temple gates, was seen.

"How would it be now if I seize the goddess Manuhari?" he respectfully inquired of the sage. The sage declaimed, "If you are going to seize her, seize her!" When the hunter cast the efficacious jewel sling, he caught the goddess Manuhari by the right hand, and all her comrades flew off into the sky. Then Manuhari thought thus to herself, 'A sinful hunter has seized me among us many maidens at the lake where the Esrua-gods gather and wash. If he lays hand on me, because my person is pure and immaculate, I shall die," she thought. Giving him her own fine jeweled ring, she said, "Take this and let me go. If you take this jeweled ring, it is [worth] more than all the goods of the Jambudvipa-continent. I am unable to be the mate of an ordinary mortal. I am of noble and pure origin, and immaculate."

The hunter said, "Although you may die, I shall not send you to your land. If I seize you with the efficacious sling, it will work." He wrapped her hands doubled with the efficacious sling, and when she was biting the riverbank and getting a toehold on stones, Manuhari thought to herself, "No matter what I may do, this man is not going to release me. If he does not release me, this small jewel encrusted in my jeweled diadem is more than all the goods of the Jambudvipa-continent. Specifically, my life-soul is within it. You take it! I can fly by the power of it. As long as you hold me, this jeweled diadem is not something of mine. Although I think of my diadem, you will surely catch me."*

When he managed to lay hand on her, the sage declaimed, "Hunter, because you are of lowly birth, it will not do for you to lay hand on her. As for the jeweled diadem, because it is Manuhari's life-soul, take it." Thereupon the hunter took the diadem, and when he stepped to a spot seven paces away, Manuhari went to a spot seven paces behind the hunter. Then the sage, the girl Manuhari, and the hunter, all three, went to the Guuri cliff. While they were dwelling there, Manuhari thought to herself, "I am devoid of a destiny, but I was born a daughter of the Kinnara King. Although there are many girls who come thus to the lake where Esrua-gods gather, a sinful man of low birth has seized me from among all of them," she thought to herself. The hunter was thinking to himself as follows. "Although a lowly fellow like me has seized such a beautiful goddess as Manuhari, if I lay hand on her, she will die," he thought.

The sage was aware of the thoughts of these two and spoke to the hunter. "If you were to give this goddess Manuhari in marriage to the prince named Manibhadra, son of King Nomci of Tabun Togo-suqsen of the north, she will surely be a queen superior to all queens. There surely cannot be found a better husband for Manuhari in the lands of man than this prince. He will surely enrich you, hunter, with goods and cattle," he said.

"If a hunter lays hand on Manuhari, she will die. Prior to this, when I followed the sage's command, my affairs resolved themselves. Now, too, let it be in accord with the sage's command," he said. Seizing Manuhari's jeweled diadem himself, he had Manuhari follow and they went to the palace of Prince Manibhadra of Tabun Togo-suqsen of the north. With the prince's minister as matchmaker, he brought Manuhari and came before the king.

The hunter made obeisance, and placed the jeweled diadem in the king's hand, and said respectfully as follows:

> Oh powerful heavenly prince, hear ye!
> I manifestly present to be married as queen

* This passage of Manuhari's thoughts is obscure.

> This Manuhari, daughter of the incomparable Kinnara;
> No more beautiful one is there in the world.

The prince and Manuhari marveled one at the other, and looked one another over this way and that. Prince Manibhadra thought to himself as follows. "Although I have 500 wives, when I look at her, they are like apes. Such a queen of mine as she has surely come by strength of merit."

Thereupon, when they made an extremely joyous feast, the prince's glory and majestic refulgence fell on Manuhari, and Manuhari's glory and majestic refulgence fell on the prince, and owing to the luminence of them both, the palace shone like bronze, gleaming and sparkling. The prince bestowed a large state on the huntsman.

As the (new) king and queen dwelt, constantly happy together, his five hundred wives thought thus to themselves, "Since this Manuhari came, the prince has neither looked nor glanced at us." And they all talked together. "Let us devise a means to do away with this Manuhari," they said.

The father of the prince, King Nomci, had a magician, a lama named Qara Qari (Somber Stranger). The five hundred wives flattered (?) this lama with goods, and said as follows. "Since this Manuhari came, the prince does not even glance at us. Lama, work out a way to dispose of her," they said. This sage went and spoke to the Maharaja Nomci.

"Oh Maharaja! Since the prince is replete with might and main, if he should go and lead an army against our protagonist, the enemy in the south, he surely would be able to defeat them. Now, if one does not utilize this prince's might, the enemy may later vanquish us with their strength, and it might happen that we would lose our kingdom," he said.

The king loved his son and did not send him. When the sage repeatedly mentioned it, the king appointed Prince Manibhadra head of the northern army and was about to send him [into battle]. When it was time for the army to depart, Prince Manibhadra thought to himself as follows. "The king has verily given a command; now there is naught else [to do] but to go," he said, and his face grew gloomy. As he sat there, Manuhari said to the prince,

> Son of Heaven, insatiable to behold,
> Savior of sentients by a sublimely sage scheme,

> Whereas previously your visage was manifestly bright,
> Why is your bright countenance overcast today?

The prince declaimed, "My supremely beautiful Manuhari, hear ye! My father's command is grave. The army of the north and I are to go. How am I to go and leave you?" he said. Manuhari said, "Manibhadra, beautifully imbued with complexion and vigor, hear ye! It is not possible to break the king's command. If you are to go with the northern army, as planned, how am I to dwell separated from you? Now give me my jeweled diadem and send me to the land of the Kinnara. I shall make a wish for us to meet later," she said.

The prince did not agree, but went and took Manuhari in to his mother the queen, and reported to his mother, "Until I return from the army, do you, mother, supervise this diadem and Manuhari. Give her the diadem when harm threatens her life. Do not give it for any other reason," he said, and had his mother keep the diadem and Manuhari.

He went into the army. Later, the wily sage Qara Qari discovered a way, and had King Nomci dream an evil dream. He made him dream that he went to a place and his insides were taken out, that his stomach was wrapped up three times, and that his heart was taken out. When the king asked the sage for an interpretation, the sage spoke. "The king is in danger of dying. Set up a filled pool before the royal palace, and in it fix a four-step podium of stone. On this, anoint Kinnara fat, and the king is to wash in the water. Then make a fragrance with Kinnara girl fat, and when the king comes out on this podium, have a man versed in the eight Brahmanic wisdoms lick his feet, and the harmful demon will come out."

The king declaimed, "Where is one to find Kinnara fat?" and the sage Qara Qari said, "Is not the king's daughter-in-law a Kinnara?" The king declaimed, "I have sent Manibhadra, who is like my own heart, to the army. If I slay Manuhari, who is like Manibhadra's own eyes, how am I to remain alive?" he said.

The sage said, "For the sake of your life, if you love the daughter-in-law more than your own life, I am unable to effect a cure." The king believed the sage's statement, and Manuhari, hearing that she was to be taken to make a cure, said to the Queen Mother, "The Maharaja is being deceived by the sage Qara Qari. Pretending it necessary, they are going to slay me. Please give me my diadem. I shall return," she said.

When the queen mother looked furtively from the palace window, she saw the executioner coming and was afraid, and placing the jeweled diadem in Manuhari's hand, said, "Go quickly!" Manuhari took the diadem and flew up into the sky, saying to the executioner, "Oh most mighty forces, hear ye! The Maharaja has been deceived by others. Harm befell the life of blameless Manuhari. If you desire Manuhari's fat, come up in the sky," she said and flew away.

Beginning with the king, they all repented together. They repented greatly together, saying "What are we to say when Prince Manibhadra comes and inquires, 'Where has Manuhari gone?'" The sage Qara Qari said, "Oh King, indeed evil and obstacles have manifestly emerged."

Then the goddess Manuhari said, "When I was formerly in the grotto of Guuri cliff, good and evil deeds came to pass there. Let me go there, meet that former sage, and relate my tale," she said and went. Bowing to the prior sage, she said as follows:

> We, Sage, Naga and Hunter, after resolving our differences,
> Encountered the prince by the might of pure destiny;
> A youth so greatly beloved would not leave [me], we thought;
> Because the beneficent Maharaja was deceived by others.
>
> After good Manibhadra went into the army,
> The girls all but brought harm to my fine life;
> The queen mother gave me my unequalled diadem;
> Without delay I was to go to the land of the Kinnaras.
>
> This bejeweled ring,
> At the time when the mighty prince came to sue for me,
> I gave to him, and said* these words,
> "We two shall surely meet by the might of ancient destiny."
>
> Beyond a land some leagues from here
> Is a lake where Esrua-gods gather and wash;
> In a country beyond this noble lake
> Lies a boundless dense forest.
>
> Within it are many jewels of all sorts,
> Shielding the heavens, sun and moon;
> In a land some leagues beyond it
> Are manifest carnivores on a snowclad mountain.
>
> It is not possible to endure the unbearable cold;
> In a land some leagues beyond that,
> On the other hand, the danger of serpents is great;
> To such a yonder land I arrived.

---

* The 'let it be said!' (*oguuletugei*) of the text seems to be a *lapsus* for the simple past (*oguulebei*).

There poisonous water boils up to the sky;
Constantly the poison water flows and trickles;
If one comes to a land beyond here
There are harmful insects like long-nosed flies, bees and so forth.

There are also large hosts of *pretas* (?) which are disagreeable;
When one comes to the land not far beyond this,
It is our superior Kinnara land;
Its palace is lofty and very majestic.

At its top is a white canopy, and its peak is beautiful;
In the corners it is finely netted about with pearls;
There are four superior lakes for washing, in the four directions;
There are many different flowers delighting all.

There are many treasuries of gold, silver and jewels;
There are also many carnivores like lions and others;
In compassion they bring no harm to one another,
And are in company with whatever offspring be there.

In wintertime, fruit and flowers appear from trees;
In such an esteemed and sublime land
I, Manuhari, am thinking of thee, master;
Amongst my many unbounded comrades my thought is on thee.

On account of such fearful things, you surely will be unable to come from there. If you come after me without fear of those intervening horrors,

May you come enumerating these various things!
Here in a land some leagues beyond
There is a lake where Esrua-gods gather and wash;
Please come after washing with such esteemed water!

There in a land some leagues beyond

There is a transparent flat white crystal;
If you come carrying it wholly on your shoulder,
Its efficiency will protect you from the danger of carnivores.
In a land some leagues beyond there

There is a well-inaugurated white pagoda
Of the Well-Gone Kasyapa Buddha;
When you have bowed to it, circumambulated and taken the
    blessing,
Within this incomparable pagoda

There is superior kashika-fabric.
When you take it quickly, load it on your shoulders and proceed,
It delivers you from the angry carnivores of the snowclad mountains.
If you go to a land further beyond

There is an elephant fashioned from stone.
Beneath the stone elephant is an iron hammer.
If you take the hammer resolutely, and strike the elephant's belly,
The essence of it is that there is an immortal spring which fills jugs.

If you partake of it and anoint your person,
It manifestly delivers [one] from poison water and harmful serpents.
When you come to a land beyond this,
There is the palace of the incomparable Kinnara King.

I, captivating Manuhari, in that Land
Shall dwell, thinking well on thee;
Unrivaled prince,
Please proceed to that land without delay.

With such words of instruction did she command the sage, and flew away to her own land.

Thereupon Prince Manibhadra vanquished all the enemies of the north, and returned. Owing to the fact that the Maharaja and all the others had been deceived by the sage Qara Qari, they said, "Manuhari has returned to her own country." The prince's mind was sorely troubled, and his father the Maharaja declaimed, "I shall give you to wife a human girl far superior to Manuhari." He replied, "Where can there be found one like Manuhari who was perfected in all the signs, pure and immaculate among the Kinnara women?"

Since this has entered the mind of each and every such one, neither woman, duck, thief nor monks who bestrive their strivings will repose. On account of such the Maharaja and all the others could not restrain the prince. Then after the prince had departed to seek her, seeing that the moon of the fifteenth had come out, he wondered to himself as follows:

Oh Moon, king of the stars which have filled your destiny,
As you go, revolving quickly over the four continents,

> Hast thou seen in the world the fair and beautiful Manuhari,
> Finer than all, with eyes like the lotus leaf?

Then going to a yonder country, and mindful of how they had formerly been happy together, he saw an antelope-doe and wondered to himself as follows:

> Oh you nicely sympathetic antelope,
> Go in peace eating grass and water.
> I am no vicious hunter.
> Have you seen the well-behaved Manuhari, she of the fine doe eyes?

Then he went to a further country, and perceiving a bee on a flower amidst many flower-gardens, he wondered to himself as follows:

> Oh gatherer in gardens and reeds
> The color of honeybees and indigo,
> Have you clearly perceived in the world
> The long jet-black-haired one with the wasp-waist by herself?

When he went on, he saw a serpent, and wondered to himself,

> Oh producer of poison from mouth and snout,
> Flashing your tongue like a tree leaf,
> There is no one of such bad habit and vicious lust as you.
> Have you seen the incomparable Manuhari?

Then going to a further country, he perceived the singing of a fine cuckoo bird, and again he asked himself:

> Oh dweller in the top of trees like larch and others,
> You cuckoo, king of all birds,
> Have you glimpsed Manuhari
> The lotus-eyed, more beautiful than all?

When he came to a further country, seeing a tree which had spread out many blossoms, he wondered and asked:

> Oh assemblage of trees of fortune and sanctity
> You have become the king of trees and plants.
> Dispel my melancholy quickly and well.
> Have you seen the intellect-ravishing Manuhari?

When they all of them gave no reply, the prince thus thought to himself: "Now as to when Manuhari is coming back, there is nothing else [to do] but to ask the sage, when I meet him, how it will be," he said. Arriving before the sage at Cliff Guuri, he bowed to him and said respectfully as follows:

> Dweller in the style of Gautama
> In the grotto of the cliff called Guuri,
> Reflector of Gautama's doctrine,
> Have you seen the stone-like Manuhari?
>
> Oh thinker on the Diamond Vehicle (=Vajrayana)
> By diamond-like firm thought
> In the grotto of the diamond-like cliff,
> Hast thou seen the Diamond-*Dakini*-like Manuhari?

The sage said, "When Manuhari went back, she stopped past here, and said, 'Let this be given to the prince as a bequest!' and bestowed a jeweled ring."

> "I have presented a ring to the prince's hand.
> The prince and I, we two, were intimate comrades in this rebirth.
> By the malice of persons of evil design
> I left and went to my own country.

Now it is not necessary to pursue me. Because there are many great dangers in the intervening places, it will not be possible for you, a mortal of the Jambudvipa-continent, to attain the country of the Kinnara. Take this ring and return.' This was Manuhari's command," he said.

The prince spoke. "Even if it is a matter of my life, I am going to seek Manuhari," he said, and was on the point of going. The sage said, "If this prohibition is not obeyed, and the prince is going to go, these are Manuhari's instructions previously to the sage on the means of evading these dangers." The sage instructed the prince in detail. The prince, by virtue of both performing and executing these things, arrived at the land of the Kinnara king.

Then when he saw a lovely girl carrying a jeweled jug of water on her back, he inquired of this maiden, "What are you going to do with this water?" She said, "Our comrade Manuhari went to wash in the water where the Esrua assemble and wash. A sinful hunter from amongst the humans has seized her. She is to wash with the water his filth which adhered to her." The prince declaimed, "Does she wash letting this water flow in gushes, or does she wash letting it pour all at once?" "She will wash letting it flow in gushes," she said. Thereupon the prince, unbeknownst to yonder girl, cast the ring into the jar. The girl now took the water and went, and when she poured it all at once, all the impurities were to come off.

The girl took the water and went, and when Manuhari washed, she poured it without letting it gush. Seeing the ring which fell out, she marveled, and inquired of the girl. The girl said, "There was a man standing by the water's edge." Manuhari jumped, descending from the high steps and leaping from the low steps, and ran hastily. Seeing the prince, she took him by the hand and reported as follows:

> Oh prince who is like my inmost heart, hear ye!
> Have you come after defeating the enemies of the north?
> Has the sage of true command conveyed my words to you?
> Have you arrived safely, steadily evading the dangers
>   on the way?

The prince declaimed,

> Thinking of you, peerless Manuhari,
> I said, 'Let me pursue her however difficult the deeds';
> When the sage conveyed your instruction to me
> I came and arrived here in tranquility, desiring you.

Then Manuhari invited him to her own palace filled with treasures of the five wishes, and as they dwelt nicely enjoying themselves, the prince declaimed: "Report to the king your father that I shall now return and take you home. My father and mother, the king and queen, are surely greatly worried," he said. Manuhari went and spoke respectfully as follows to the king of the Kinnara.

"Oh King my father, if Manibhadra from the land of men were to arrive here, what would you do, oh King?" she inquired. The king declaimed, "If that man comes to this land, I shall surely cut him into one hundred and eight pieces." She declaimed, "Oh King, in the realm of man a hunter of low station took hold of me. At that time, Prince Manibhadra took me to wife and loved me greatly," she said. The King's anger and wrath became tranquil, and he said, "If Prince Manibhadra comes here, I shall adorn you nicely and regale him with many goods and a thousand Kinnara maidens, and give you in betrothal."

Manuhari rejoiced, and adorning the prince nicely with divine ornaments, she gave him jewels and so forth, and many goods. When he met the king and made presents of these, the king came and received him at the central gate, they met together, and he seated him on the great high throne. He entertained him nicely with tasty food and drink. They conducted talks for a month in harmony with doctrine. When the prince reported, "Please deign to bestow Manuhari on me. I shall be going back," the Kinnara king declaimed, "Although the numerous suitors included the god Khormusta and others, because she was so greatly beloved by me, I did not bestow her. I shall not give her to you."

In order to have the prince display his manhood, they set up a group of a seven-fold golden tree, a seven-fold palm tree, a seven-fold drum and seven-fold swine, and when they had the prince shoot, the prince shot through them all with a single arrow. He chopped through them all at once with his blue-lotus leaf sword. Then the Kinnara king marveled greatly, and said, "On the day after tomorrow, early, I shall send a thousand identical maidens, headed by Manuhari. If you are able to recognize Manuhari from among them, take her." When he sent them in that wise, the prince prayed a holy invocation to himself: "If my wish which I have thought is to be fulfilled, let the goddess Manuhari emerge ahead of the thousand maidens at the space of one fathom," he said. Manuhari came out ahead of the many maidens, and then the king bestowed Manuhari on the prince.

Making a grand feast, they beheld great spectacles. He presented a dowry of cintamani-jewels and other jeweled things, silks and silk-stuffs, male and female servants; for a retinue, a thousand maidens, elephants, horses, water buffalos and other livestock as a favor. The Kinnara king and his company of comrades accompanied Manuhari and the prince as far as the Esrua assembly lake. They discussed doctrine exclusively for two or three sun-rounds and were in fine agreement. Then when the time came for Manuhari and the prince to go, the Kinnara king's thoughts were greatly moved, and speaking to Manuhari as follows, he gave these admonitory commands:

> Relying on the might of the Jewel Prayer,
> You were born and became my lawful descendant;
> Being extremely beautiful and with perfected senses,
> Hear ye now your father's admonitions.

We of the race of Gandharvas
Have unerringly been purified from harmful impediment;
Because of believing in the liberating Three Jewels,
Carry out your faith with thoughts devoid of harm.

Strive well and unimpededly for the splendor of doctrine;
Abandon sin and confusion from afar;
Eschew boasting, calumny and gossip;
Reject envy of your peers.

Spare not your life as regards the splendor of sublime merit;
Contrariwise, avoid sin even if minor;
Worship well the unrivaled clergy;
Perform not the ten sins through stupidity.

Worship well the Buddha (statues) and the excellent temple;
Read unceasingly the unparalleled doctrine;
It delivers [one] from the dangers of malicious demons;
My beautiful daughter, this is my admonition.

Now having found such a fine rebirth, and
Becoming the queen of a mighty king,
You are surrounded with nation and ruling ministers,
Men and women, kith and kin.

Rich in cattle and possessions,
Vanquishing enemies by various means,
In a jeweled city without equal,
You eat delicious food and enjoy yourself.

When the lord of death comes, it will be of no use;
If you truly believe in the Three Jewels,
They will save you from sorrow;
I have taught you these things constantly in accord with doctrine.

Now I shall instruct you in the ways of the world.
When you go from here to the land of mortals,
To be agreeable with all at that time is the best of actions;
If you perform altruisms, don't always say, "I accomplished that."

However wise you yourself may be,
Do not humiliate lesser and lower beings;
However acute your intellectual wisdom may be,
You must always investigate every matter.

Although they are not as beautiful as you

> Hearken to the words of simple and plain folk;
> Although the assistance is your own property,
> By unstinting when helping and giving to others;
> Give up all base ways and means, which are barriers.
>
> Act in one manner, neither openly nor concealed;
> Satisfy the folk with food and drink;
> Do not call openly for the restraint of others;
> Perform all deeds carefully alone.
>
> However many people be gathered,
> Defend those both near and far alike;
> If you praise yourself falsely, and denigrate others,
> It is reason for you to become a laughingstock to all people.
>
> These are my admonitions which I have instructed,
> Beginning from now, and no matter when,
> Constantly heed these my words! My Manuhari,
> It will be difficult for me to meet you again.

When he had instructed her and spoken so, Manuhari took the king by the hand and stated these words in reply.

> Oh my father the king, who is the supreme one of Gandharvas (sic),
> Of illumined lineage and with might and strength,
> Who well vanquished the evil enemies beyond,
> Hear ye well these my words in your refulgence.
>
> When we were born from the womb, and
> When we were small, you plied us with sweets and trinkets,
> Loving us like the apple of your eye,
> Supreme Kinnara king, my father, please attend this!
>
> I am leaving behind myself everything,
> Brothers and sisters, kind parents,
> Beloved comrades and all my people, and
> My unsurpassed Kinnara palace.
>
> Am I to go to an unknown land?
> When I consider I shall be looking at the faces of unknown and inconsequential people,
> Truly I will think even more on transience.
> It will constantly touch my thoughts.
>
> Abandoning now my good happiness like this
> I shall now go to a land of uncouth humans;

> Though a girl be of lowly lineage
> If her complexion and family be fine, she provokes discord.
>
> When a girl is of fine appearance,
> If she is nicely equipped with many virtues,
> She will fall into the hands of inconsequential persons;
> I have been thinking of the shortness and transience of life.
>
> When the sea evaporated and dried up from heat, my mind was not at rest.
> When all the crops were beaten by hail, I was unbelieving.
> When the marvelous flowers were taken by the cold, my color greatly changed.
> Alas! Alack! My heart is greatly moved.

A girl having gone to the land to which she is sent will dwell in the land where she has been settled. May malicious harm and evil not touch (her) precious body, and may she be forever firm and steady like Mount Sumeru!

> I, the girl named Manuhari,
> Devoid of harm and evil to my body,
> Fulfilling your command without fail, went to the land of man.
> May it be for certain that I again meet with my father!

The men and women of the Kinnara king's retinue bowed to Manuhari, and reported as follows:

> Supreme one of gods and men,
> Greatly luminous one like the unrivaled sun and moon,
> Like the cintamani that fulfills the wishes of sentients without hesitation,
> Like the kalpavrksa-tree that produces in a manifest way goods,
>
> Like a wish-fulfilling fruit, when you satisfy perfect desires,
> Have we praised you, our own beautiful girl.
> You will go to the foreign land by the force of prior prayers;
> Our hearts have been greatly troubled.
>
> When you go to the foreign land,
> In full view of king and people, ever like a topmost adornment,
> Defend like a descendant the entire people brought together;
> May that whole land be filled with fortune and sanctity!

When they said this, Manuhari uttered her reply:

> All of ye were variously born to the Kinnara lineage
> By the power of ancient destiny, and were happy;
> Now ye all have seen and instructed me;
> Be it that we meet again in a rebirth after this one!

Then grasping Prince Manibhadra by the hand, the Kinnara king spoke as follows in verse:

> Oh great splendid and majestic one of bodhi-thought,
> Ornamented with numerous virtues among many existing men,
> Vanquisher by glory of the wicked enemy,
> Oh Bodhisattva youth, hear ye henceforth!
>
> Specifically as for this Manuhari, who is my descendant,
> In her are perfected the supremely good signs;
> Though mighty ones of the world clearly desired her,
> Considering your wish alone have I given her.
>
> Leaving her kind parents and others,
> Henceforth only you, her beloved husband, will she follow.
> Ever love her, and do not torment her;
> Lo! Though she be foremost, she must heed your words.
>
> At the time when the evil dark sage
> Did harm to Manuhari's person,
> Did not Manuhari escape all right by her own wits?
> Remember these my words without fail, Oh Prince!

The prince declaimed to the Kinnara king:

> By the might of punya performed of old
> Reborn now as king of the Kinnara,
> Worshipping the Three Jewels as the topmost ornament,
> Lord and King of the Kinnara, hear ye!
>
> I am the prince without compare of the land of men;
> I requested Manuhari from you by the might of a pure
>   invocation;
> We are to be reborn together in each and every rebirth;
> Oh, why should I cause torment when I go from here?

Saying this, they grasped one another's hands, prayed a holy prayer to meet again later, and the Kinnara king returned.

Resplendent Prince Manibhadra and Queen Manuhari, in company with all their comrades, proceeded to the delightful palace called *Tabun togolder* in the north. All the people of that land were aware that Prince Manibhadra was coming, and coming from afar brought music, cymbals, drums, canopies, banners ("victorious tokens") and so forth. They met and bowed before them many times, and reported, saying as follows:

> Suppressor of inimical demons, defender of the king's realm,
> Prince who has become the refuge of many sentients,
> After going to the land of the Kinnara, not desolate,
> Have you returned well and safe from the various intervening dangers?

So they said, and the prince declaimed,

> Hear ye, oh my many assembled people!
> When the army and I went in the north,
> [I thought] I had delivered fair Manuhari from the hands of the executioner,
> But I had to perform many difficult deeds before I found her and returned to you.

The reception committee bowed to Manuhari and said and praised as follows:

> You have become an ornament among all goddesses;
> It is evident that you have made all rejoice by pure deeds;
> You who create happiness for sentients by unstinting thought;
> Wondrous Manuhari, have you arrived healthy and well?

Manuhari declaimed;

> Having acquired a precious and irrevocable human rebirth,
> In this land in which Buddhism is so greatly disseminated,
> The great sainted King and Queen, ministers and entire people
> Are all indeed very fine at the present time.

Prince Manibhadra and Manuhari arrived at the perfectly happy land called Tabun Togolder, and when he had bowed to his own father and mother, the king and queen, those two said, "We have been saying that Prince Manibhadra perished in the intervening interval." Their minds in addition had been very troubled, but when they arrived safely, the king and queen were very happy, and then his father the king said to the prince as follows:

> The prince called Sain Cindamani (Good Wish-Jewel)
> Is indeed more rare than the blossom of the incomparable
>   wild-fig.
> My prince who vanquished enemies of yonder unimpededly
> Is more rare than the lord of fine armies.*
>
> Manibhadra who is wise in comprehension and wisdom
> Is more rare than the fortuned minister jewel.
> My Manibhadra of tranquil mind devoid of wrath and anger
> Is more rare than the high and mighty elephant jewel.
>
> My Manibhadra who goes swiftly by magical transformation
> Is more rare than a fair and beauteous horse jewel.
> My Manibhadra who guided by reins the whole nation
> Is rare far more than a wheel jewel.
>
> My Manibhadra, whom one looks at insatiably after he arrived,
> Is more rare than the queen jewel who engenders happiness upon
>   bestowal.
> Now Manibhadra and Manuhari have arrived here healthy and
>   well,
> Beginning from today and forever your parents' minds will be
>   very peaceful.

Then the prince reported as follows to his two parents:

> My parents, who superiorly fashioned my body,
> Praising and worshipping forever,
> May your life be firm and unchanging,
> May you be reborn as my parents in more future rebirths!

Then Manuhari uttered an invocation as follows:

> When you three, father, mother and son, are together, and
> When we manifestly become friendly in many rebirths,
> May I, Manuhari, in many rebirths there,
> Be reborn as your queen beyond all doubt.

When she had prayed such a holy invocation, the entire people of the north became extremely rich in goods, field crops came forth in large number, plague and disease vanished, and all the people had long life.

* Emended from *ceceq* "blossoms" to *cereq* "armies" on the basis of the Vessantarajataka.

At that time Prince Manibhadra sat upon the regal throne, and for twelve years to the entire great people bestowed alms of doctrine and presented alms of goods, and made the whole nation greatly rejoice.

"As for the king and father of that time, it was the king my father Pure Food (Suddhodana) of the present day. My mother of that time is my mother Mahamaya of the present time. If we mention the Kinnara king, the Horse-Headed One (Hayagriva) of that time, it is Sakya with Staff in Hand of the present time.

"The Manuhari of that time is the Sakya Maid who protects the earth of the present time. And as for Prince Manibhadra of that time, it is indeed I, Sakyamuni of the present time.

"The sage in the grotto of Guuri Cliff of that time is Sariputra of the present time. As regards the hunter of those days, it is Maudgalyayana of the present day. The sage Qari Qari of that time becomes various different persons, and is now the Black Shimnus Vevanta," he said.

This tale of Good Manibhadra, from the sutra composed by *Obosu-ben Boluqsan Ochir* ("Self-Origin Vajra") and *Uxani Ildu* ("Sword of Intellect"), Zasaqtu Qung Taiji commanded "Translate it into Mongolian!".

Pandita Kuo-shih translated it into the Mongolian dialect.

The disciple named Buddhakala wrote it.

Manggalam!

Chaṅs-dbyaṅs Rgya-mcho

SELECTIONS FROM THE LOVE POETRY OF THE SIXTH DALAI LAMA

TRANSLATED BY CHARLES HARTMAN

INTRODUCTION

THE sixth Dalai Lama (1683–1707), *Chaṅs-dbyaṅs rgya-mcho* (Ocean-of-Melody) wrote the following poems. As his verses reveal, he was a rather atypical Dalai Lama. But despite his gaiety and romantic temperament, his life was basically unhappy. He died at the age of 24, a victim of Sino-Mongol-Tibetan political intrigues. Tibetan legend claims that the Chinese, on the orders of Emperor K'ang-shi, murdered him. His followers understood the reference in his poetry to Li-thaṅ as a prophecy concerning his next reincarnation. And in 1708 the seventh Dalai Lama was born in that village.

In the original Tibetan, these poems have four lines of six syllables each: the complete poem has only twenty-four syllables, and in brevity of expression resembles the twenty-character Chinese lyric (*chüeh-chü*) and the seventeen-syllable Japanese *haiku*. The oriental mind appreciates this brevity and its corresponding vagueness. Thus the reader should not be dismayed if he cannot understand the Eastern as he would a Western poem. The Tibetan author presents only the components of a poetic situation. The reader must draw upon these imagerial elements and form them himself into a personal poetic message. But an Eastern and a Western reader will doubtlessly accomplish this process differently; since, no matter how adept a translation may be, an American cannot be furnished with the mental apparatus of an eighteenth-century Tibetan. Therefore, I have chosen for translation eleven poems which transcend as far as possible the Tibetan cultural milieu. But difficulties still remain.

The sixth Dalai Lama was the spiritual leader of his country. His use of religious words or references in mundane situations enhances the novelty or "shock-value" of his poetry. Thus in the first poem, "circumambulate" translates the Tibetan custom of walking clockwise around a temple or religious site. When this pious devotion is juxtaposed in the same line with thoughts of the author's mistress, his doubtless intention was to elicit from us an indulgent smile.

The complete text containing sixty-three poems is printed in Yu Dawchyuan, *Love Songs of the sixth Dalai Lama Tshangs-dbyangs-rgya-mtsho*, Peking, 1930. The translations and introduction in this book should be used with caution and consulted only in conjunction with the review by Paul Pelliot in *T'oung Pao*, 1932 pp. 272–74.

FROM THE LOVE POETRY OF THE SIXTH DALAI LAMA

From eastern snow mountain peak
shines a clear-bright moon.
The face of an eternal beloved
circumambulates my mind.

•

A handsome peach seed,
daughter of a high official,
the ripened fruit
from heights of lofty bole.

•

If mind would tend to holy doctrine
as fast as it traces her—
this life, this very body
would I find my Buddhahood.

•

In our hide-away,
deep forest, south valleys,
only parrots squawk,
who else shall ever know?

•

Wild brant fond of the marsh
sometimes desires to settle
but ice-frozen lake surface
frustrates and despairs intent.

•

When I dwell in Potala palace
Knowledge-holding Ocean-of-Melody, I am.
When I rove in Lhasa haunts
as playboy of the Lamaist world, I'm known.

•

Dusk: "Do not arise."
Dawn: "Do not return."
Dusk: I seek my beloved.
Dawn: Snow is falling.

•

Cuckoos come from the south,
essence of seasons arrives
and I and my loved on meeting
mind and body rise to unconcern.

•

As brush of wind and rock
wear the vulture's feathers,
men's lies and men's deceits
exhaust my soul.

•

Bird, white crane,
lend me your wings.
I shall not travel far, only
encircle Li-thaṅ, then return.

•

The religion-king's magic mirror
foresees for me the hellish regions,
yet for this world I was not meant,
grant me repose in another.

THE GOBLIN K'UEI HSING

BY F. A. BISCHOFF

THE GOBLIN on page ii is K'uei Hsing 魁星, as calligraphy represents him on a stele. I purchased the rubbing in 1957, when I visited the celebrated Buddhist caves of Lung-men, south of Lo-yang.[1]

In fact it is only for reasons of homonymy that pictures of K'uei Hsing are sold at Lung-men near Lo-yang. He has nothing to do with this place. He belongs to that other Lung-men, the defile of the Yellow River in Shensi, where the southern (downstream) "gate," Yü-men-k'ou, has been opened by Yü-the-Great himself. Indeed, Lung-men near Lo-yang may be important in art history, but Lung-men in Shensi is famous in Chinese folklore—and therefore it is "the real one."

The name Lung-men, "Dragon Gate," refers to an ancient Chinese allegory. During the third moon, at the time when the peach trees are blossoming and heavy rain is falling, the carp that succeeds in swimming upstream through the rapids is instantly metamorphosed into a dragon—but only if the tail of the fish jumping out of the water is struck by lightning. The allegory, exceedingly common in Chinese literature, stands for "Success at the State Examinations."[2] Thus it is obviously proper to sell at Lung-men (it does not matter which one) pictures of K'uei Hsing, since the result of the examination depends on him. One also will notice the three dots at the right hand side of our picture: they may be interpreted as the marks juxtaposed on the examination list to the names of the three best candidates.[3]

K'uei Hsing is the arbiter of the State Examinations; he is also the god responsible for the invention, not of the principle of Chinese ideogram writing, but of the shape of the ideogram.[4] This is presumably the reason why K'uei Hsing is usually represented by a pictorial combination of ideograms. There are a great many types of such ideographic pictures, but the one shown here seems to be the classical one.

In its figurative representations, K'uei Hsing always holds a dipper (or a gold bar) in his left hand, lifts his left foot, and if space and material allow, brandishes a writing brush above his head. Among all the calligraphic representations of K'uei Hsing, the one shown on the frontispiece is the only one which faithfully follows these iconographic data developed from this *kanji* combination.[5]

The body of our K'uei Hsing is composed of four ideograms:

一正無私

They form a sentence that allows two interpretations corresponding to the above-mentioned two functions of the divinity:

"Totally right and no private [profit]," (a maxim applying to the ideal official)

and, referring to calligraphy:

"Correct at the first [touch] and no secret [corrections of the strokes]"[6]

This twofold interpretation is suggested by the colophon on the left. Taking the four ideograms one by one, the author augments them with glosses, the two first of which allude to calligraphy, the two latter referring to virtuous public officials:

一筆高擎　　正大光明
無声無臭　　私盡存誠
現奎星像　　永佇文衡

時在同治甲子春
龍泉主人敬題

洛浦漁者沐手敬繪

Totus—the brush is lifted high
Rectus—great clarity
Absque—*rumore absque odore* . . . ;
Proprio—vanishes, *servatur bonum*.

Thus appears the image of the K'uei constellation, *agentis* forever the *δημρακτικόν gubernaculum*.

THE GOBLIN K'UEI HSING   172

In the Springtime of year *Princeps* in *Commune Regimine* the lord of *Dragonici Fontis* proposed *reverentialiter* the topic.

Piscator from the bank of the Lo River purified his hands and drew *reverentialiter* the image.

And the colophon on the right reads

住持僧海雨泐石

石工劉天佑刊

The coenobite Oceanrain, the Prior, outlined the contours on the stone. The stonemason Liu T'ien-yu hewed it.

This translation is not aimed at appealing to the taste of modern readers, but at rendering the flavor of pedantic learning proper to the original: the words that are quotations are translated into Latin; Greek is used where Latin pedantry proved insufficient. The result of this experiment—a *pasticcio* of the style cherished by Renaissance humanists—comes as close as any possible to the original. But only as far as the exterior aspect is concerned. As soon as one considers the translation more in depth, it appears that it drags desperately behind because of the respective quality of Renaissance and Chinese technique of quotation: the former is superficial, the latter is artful. Even great Western humanists were perfectly satisfied when they succeeded in fitting into their own prose classical scraps regardless of the original context. On the contrary, a good Chinese quotation supposes the reader learned enough to remember at once and to recite mentally the entire passage from which the quoted words were extracted. Therefore in Chinese, the quotation is a major, an authentic tool of literary art: handled by a master it deepens the meaning to an extent unmatched, except by a few Western writers (T. S. Eliot, for example) since the Renaissance. Alas! To overlook a Chinese quotation means usually to miss the point ... our help is in the *P'ei Wen Yün Fu*, that absolutely stupendous corpus of Chinese literary quotations.[7]

As for our colophon, the three major quotations are perfectly well chosen, possess so rich a meaning that a fairly long commentary is needed to elucidate its main aspects.

• The gloss on *absque* 無 refers to the *Book of Odes* (III, I, I, 7; Legge, p. 431): "The doings of High Heaven, *Have neither sound nor smell.*" Thus the action of the mandarin is most adequately compared to the action of High Heaven.

- The gloss on *proprio* 私 is a quotation from the *Book of Changes* (Wilhelm, *The I Ching*, vol. II, pp. 12–13) with its first hemistich reworded according to the needs of the context. This allusion is so well chosen—with the "dragon" that refers to Lung-men and its allegorical meaning, the ideogram *chéng* 正 that recalls the maxim, and all the moral development outlining the ethic of the ideal official—that it deserves to be quoted *in extenso:*

> Nine in the second place means: "Dragon appearing in the field. It furthers one to see the great man." What does this signify?
> The master said: This means a man who has the character of a dragon and is moderate and *correct*. Even in ordinary speech he is reliable. Even in ordinary action he is careful. He does away with what is false and *preserves his integrity*. He improves his era and does not boast about it. His character is influential and transforms men.

My translation follows the less specific wording of Couvreur.[8]

- The ideogram *k'uei* 奎 used in the colophon is the proper designation of the eponymous star of the divinity. Yet the divinity is usually designated by another *kanji* 魁星, also pronounced *k'uei*, but combining the ideogram "demon" and the ideogram "dipper." Widely accepted folklore has confused the stars and the god and has reduced the two ideograms of *k'uei* to synonyms.[9]

- "*Agentis* forever the *gubernaculum*": this passage, obviously the pride of our glossarist, must have been felt to be incredibly beautiful:

a) K'uei Hsing is the patron of examinations, and it is certainly proper to state that "he holds forever the steelyard of Literature," or that "he is the *elegantiarum arbiter*" (to speak with Tacitus!).

b) Since the ideogram 衡 means not only "steelyard" but also "beam, handle," the author certainly intended to allude to the "handle" of the Big Dipper also. The constellation is called the Jaden Beam 玉衡

c) But the *clou*—as revealed by the *P'ei Wen Yün Fu* (p. 1140, 1)—is a twisted reference to the *Book of Odes* (II, III, IV, 2; Legge, p. 286): "The naves of [the hero Fang Shu's] wheels bound with leather, and his *yoke ornamented*." The commentators have glossed this "ornamented" with 文, "design, ornament, elegant." By changing the context, the author gave "yoke," the meaning of "steelyard" and 文 becomes "literature." The reader must forgive me if in my translation I could not move closer to the original ambiguity.

• The "year *Princeps* in *Commune Regimine*" is 1864 A.D. (The period *T'ung-Chih* ["Joint Government"] lasted from 1862 until 1874; the year *Chia-Tzu* is the first, eponymous year of the sexagenary cycle.)

• Not much can be said about the four persons mentioned in the colophons. One may assume that the rubbing was taken from a stele located in the vicinity of Lung-men near Lo-yang. In this case the "Fisherman from the Bank of the Lo River" may have been a retired *litteratus*-official[10] of the very provincial town which the once glorious Lo-yang has been for many years. But it is also possible that the stele stands at "the real" Lung-men, in Shensi, and that a modest peddler has brought the rubbings to the other Lung-men, near Lo-yang, where they can be sold. In this case, the Lo river mentioned would be the river flowing parallel to the Yellow River, a short distance to the West. Dragon Fountain can also be located in the region of Lung-men in Shensi: these is a "Market of the Dragon Fountain," Lung-chüan-chen 龍泉鎮 , located about fifty miles northwest of Yü-men-k'ou, halfway to the Lo River. Thus the "lord of the Dragon Fountain" may have been some rich man of that village.

The seal on the upper part of the rubbing presumably gives some valuable information. Unfortunately, it cannot be deciphered.

NOTES

1. A rubbing of the same stele has been published by F. E. A. Krause, "Steingravierung in Lung-mên," in the *Propyläen Weltgeschichte*, edition of 1929–1933, vol. I, p. 194. The legend of K'uei Hsing has been outlined in the foreword to this volume (p. xx). More details may be found in Henri Doré, *Recherches sur les superstitions en Chine* (Shanghai, 1914), II-ème partie, *Le panthéon chinois*, Tome VI, pp. 45 ff.; J. J. M. De Groot, *Universismus, Die Grundlage der Religion und Ethik, des Staatswesens und der Wissenschaften in China* (Berlin, 1918), pp. 286 ff.; and in the bibliographical references listed there.

2. Cf. Cor. Pétillon, *Allusions littéraires*, Variétés Sinologiques No. 13 (Shanghai, 1895), pp. 594–95. For the examination, cf. *Dai Kan-Wa Jiten*, XII, 45785, 29.

3. This, however, is only one interpretation. Professor Fred Wang, Seton Hall University, was kind enough to tell me another meaning: the picture as a whole represents the favorite divinity of the mandarins, the Big Dipper. This constellation is composed of seven stars: the four that compose the "dipper" itself are called *K'uei* 魁 星 and the three of the "handle" are called *Sho* 杓 . K'uei being represented by the goblin, the three remaining stars are shown separately by the three dots. Cf. *Dai Kan-Wa Jiten*, XII, 45785, 43. I wish to express here my gratitude to Professor Wang for his enlightening explanation.

4. Cf. the *Li Tai Ming Hua Chi* of Chang Yen-yüan as quoted by Oswald Siren, *The Chinese on the Art of Painting* (Peiping, 1936), p. 224. The above mentioned two functions of K'uei Hsing are closely related since good handwriting ("good" according to esthetical as well as graphological criteria) was a prerequisite for any of the official Chinese examinations.

5. Cf. Henri Doré in note 1. The technical term for this representation is "K'uei Hsing Kicks the Dipper" 魁星踢斗. It symbolizes "a laureate of the State Examination." Cf. *Dai Kan-Wa Jiten*, XII, 45785, 29. I owe this reference to Professor Wang also.

6. It is well known that every *kanji* stroke traced with a writing brush has to be "correct"—that means "perfectly clear"—at the "first" touch. But to the reader unfamiliar with the technique of brush writing it may be amusing to know that even a good calligrapher does not always attain "great clarity." Ordinarily the stroke turns out not to be quite as fine as expected. The disappointed artist is then tempted to mend the strokes, fattening them here and there in order to improve the balance, the proportions of his unfortunate *kanji*: these changes are precisely the "secret [corrections]" forbidden by the rules of the art. The easiest way to detect them—a method used especially by schoolteachers—consists in screening the page with the *recto* turned to the light. By observing the *verso* the corrections appear clearly as fat or lean borderlines to the body of the strokes.

7. An apparently (!) flat quotation does not weaken my argument. For the use of quotations (mainly from the *Shu Ching*) in official documents, cf. my articles, "L'Empereur de Chine, Essai sur sa situation juridique selon le point de la dynastie des T'ang," in *Collectanea Mongolica, Festchrift für Professor Dr. Rintchen*, Asiatische Forschungen, Band 17 (Wiesbaden, 1966) especially p. 26; and "Recherches sur les principes légaux des traités internationaux des T'ang," in *Studies in South, East and Central Asia presented . . . to Professor Raghu Vira*, International Academy of Indian Culture (New Delhi, 1968), especially p. 16.

8. Cf. S. Couvreur, *Dictionnaire classique de la langue chinoise; sub voc.* tch'êng.

9. Cf. Henri Doré, in note 1.

10. Fishing being in China the leisurely occupation *par excellence*, "fisherman" (cf. *P'ei Wen Yün Fu*, p. 2046, 2, and *Dai Kan-Wa Jiten*, VII, 18101, 52) became in rhetoric a synecdoche expressing all of Chinese pastoral ideals and a metaphor used for "a retired gentleman" (our *litteratus*-official), as in the celebrated *First Fu of the Red Cliff* (Zottoli, *Cursus* IV, p. 418), or by Tu Fu (as in Zach, VII, 69).